THE
PINK FAIRY BOOK

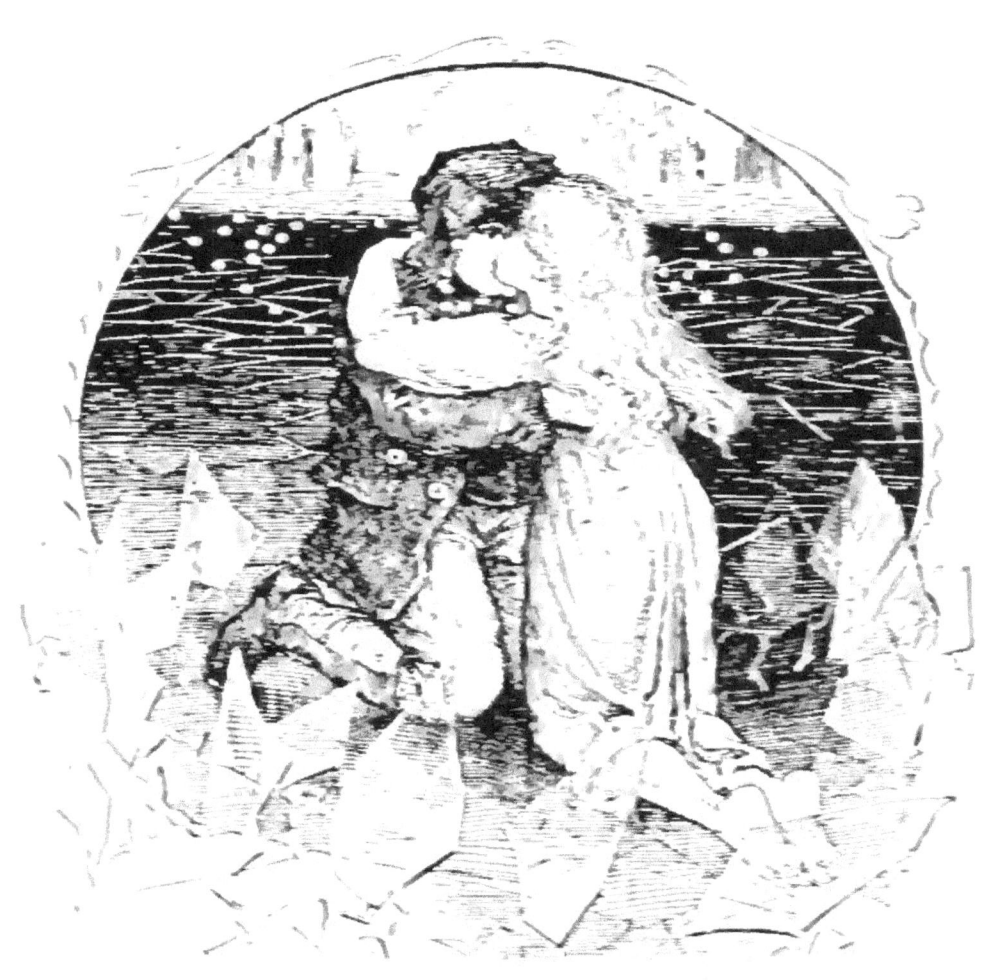

WITH NUMEROUS ILLUSTRATIONS BY H. J. FORD

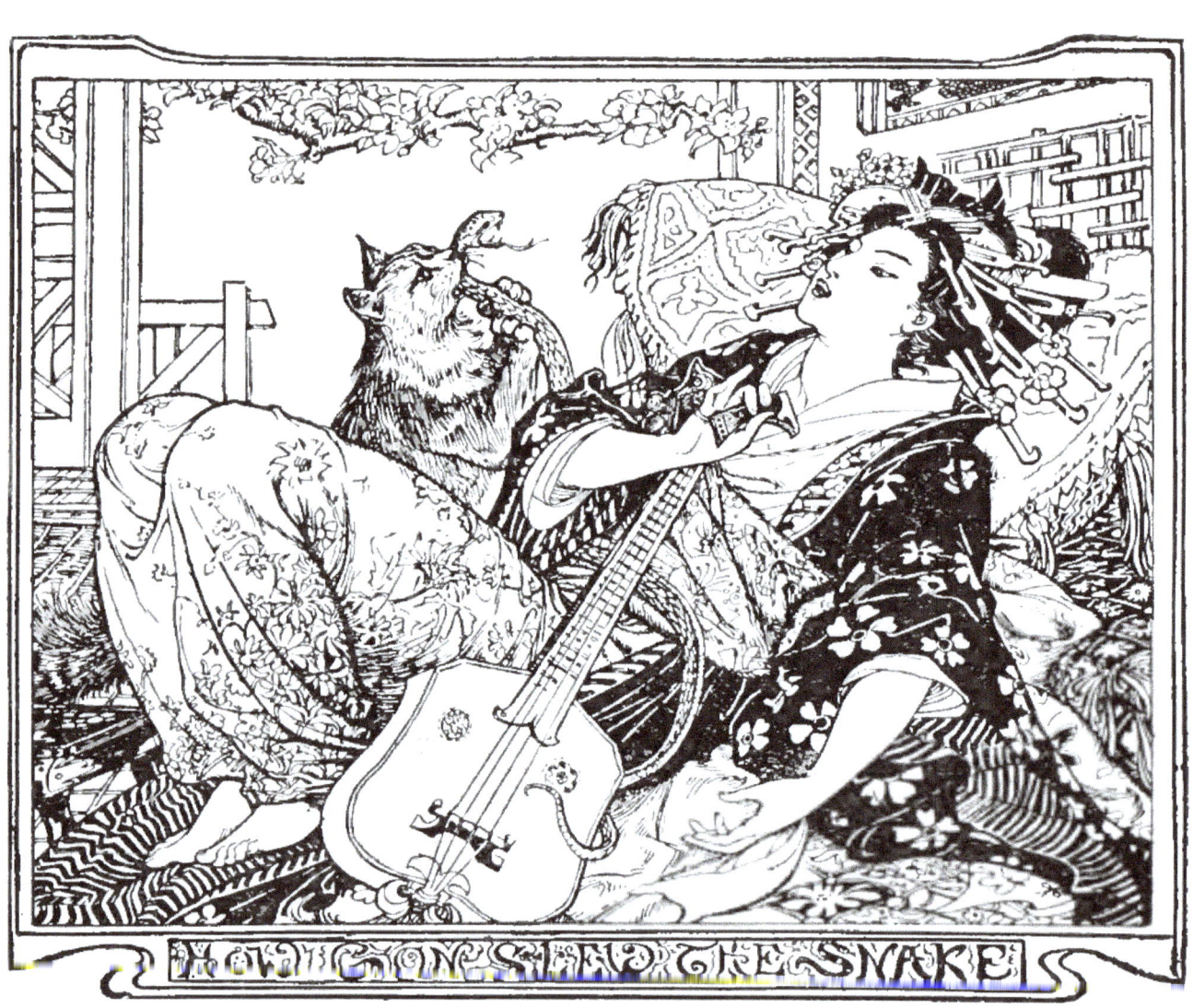
HOW TO MONSTER THE SNAKE

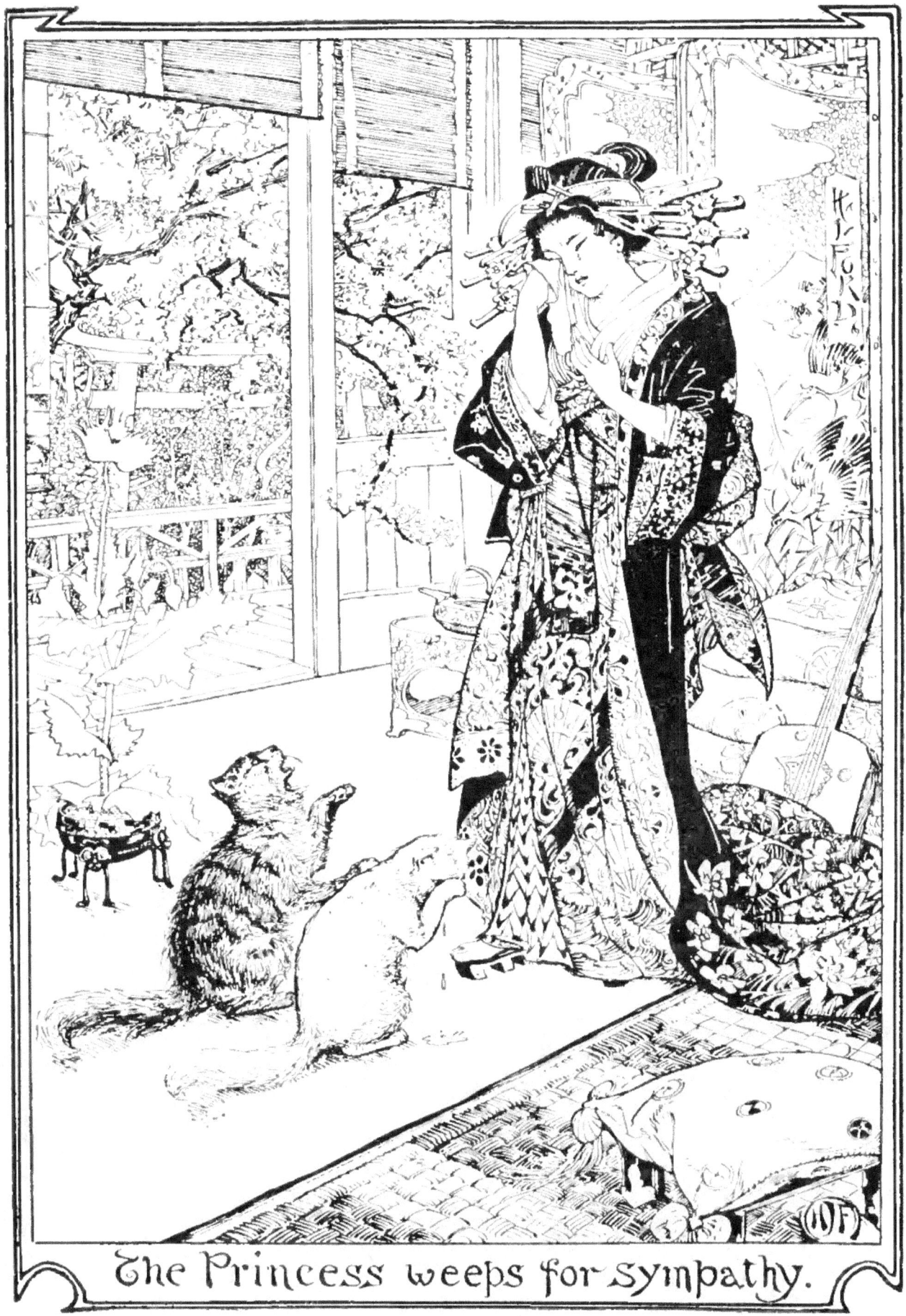

The Princess weeps for sympathy.

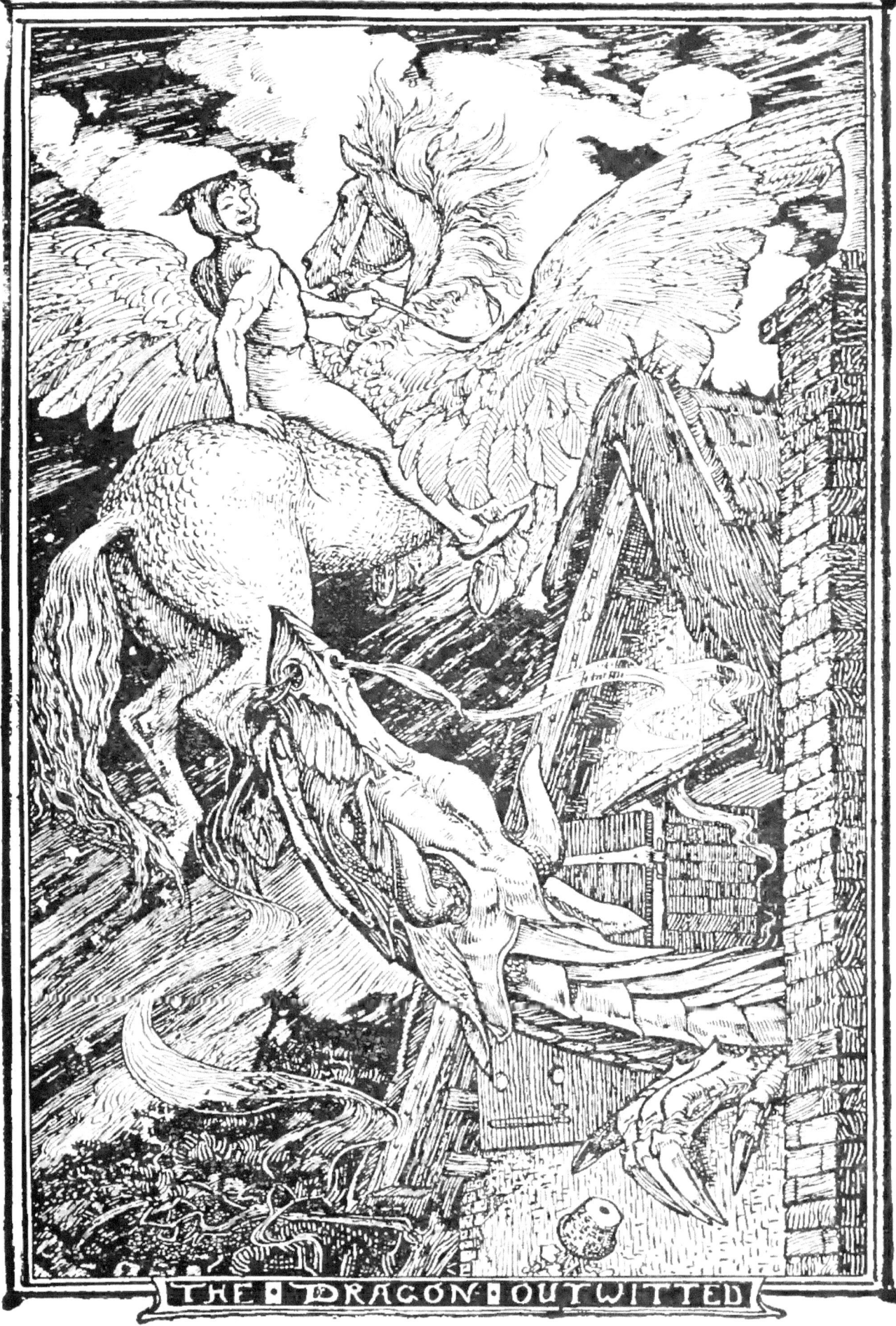

THE DRAGON OUTWITTED

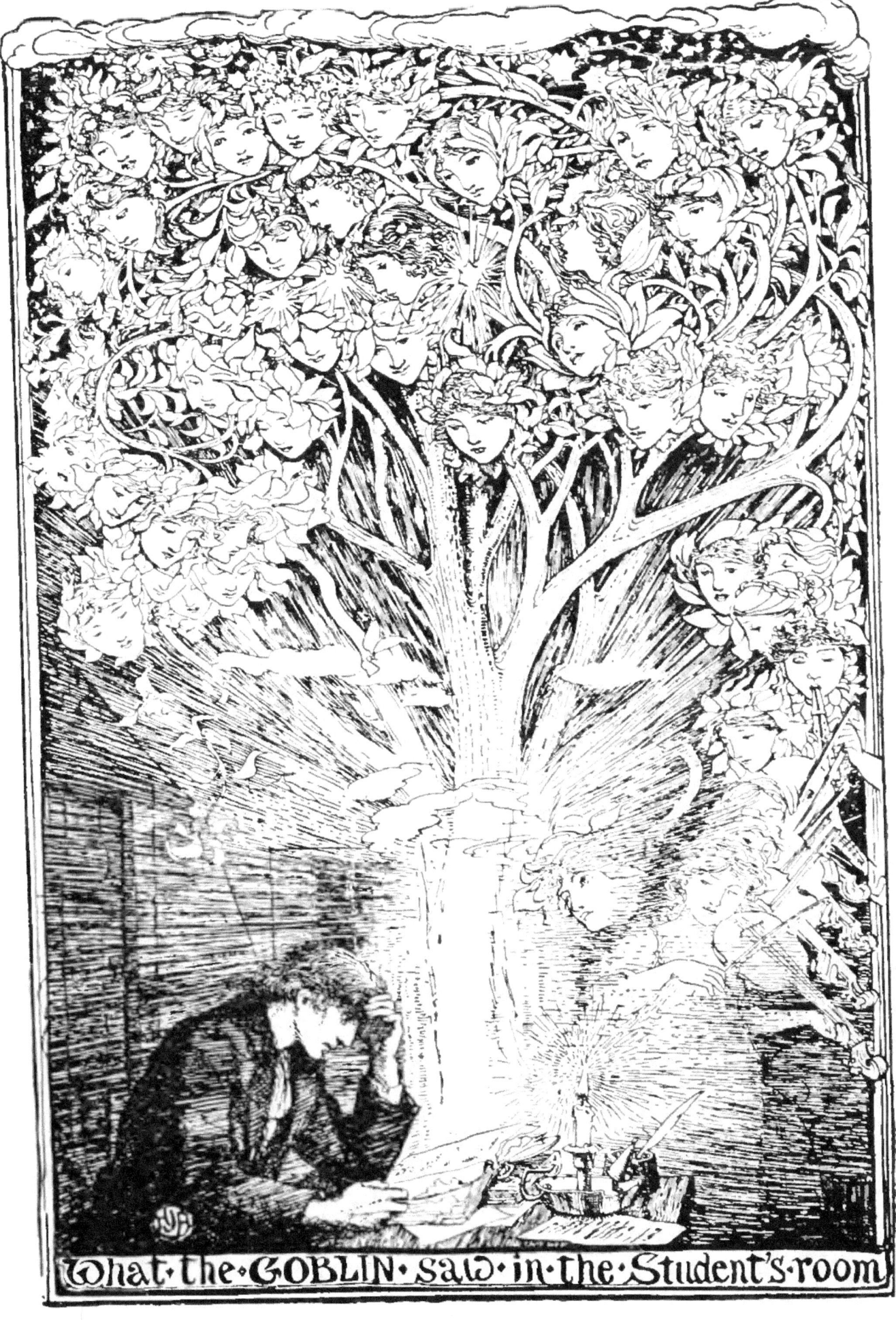

What the GOBLIN saw in the Student's room

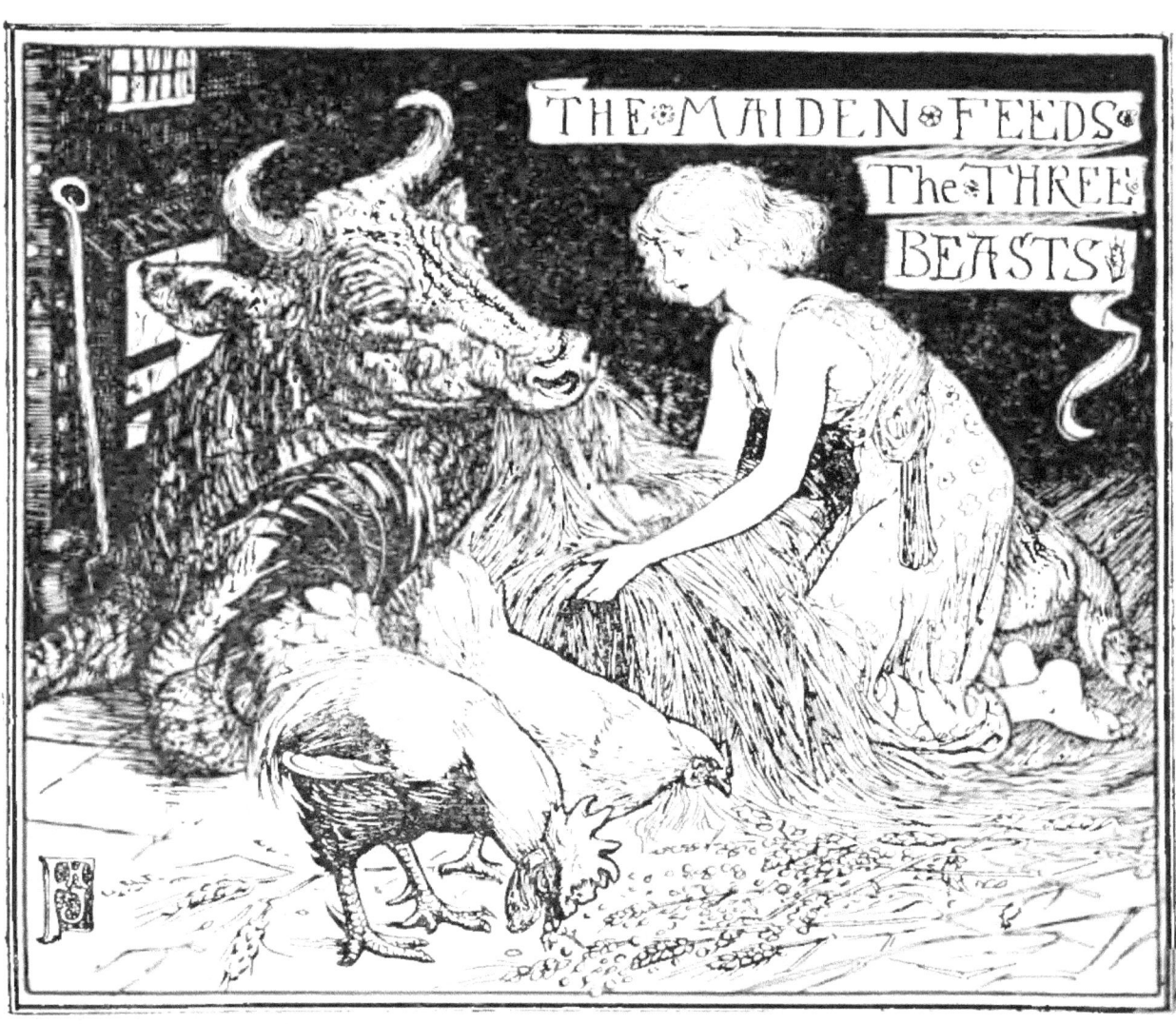

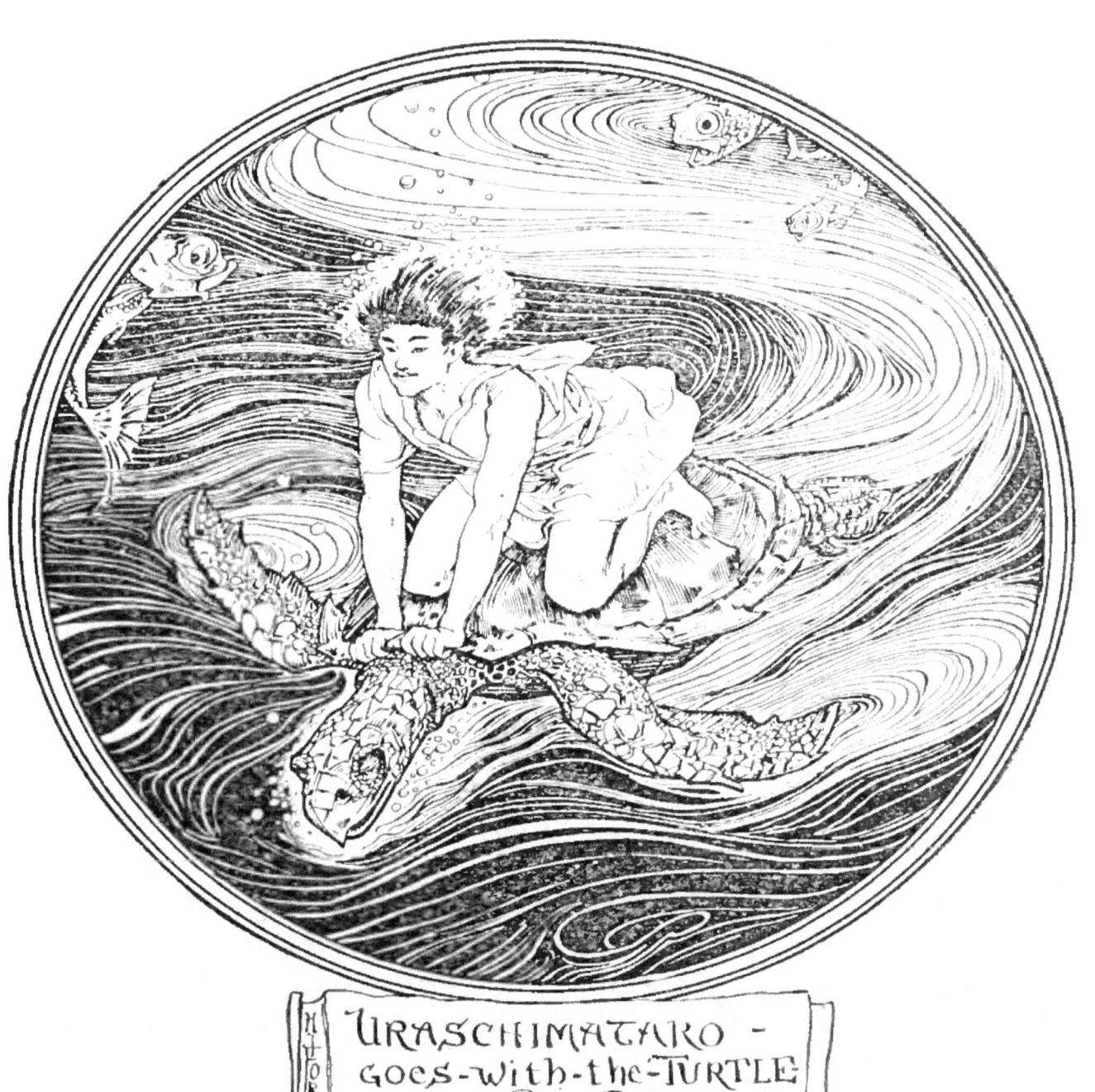

URASCHIMATARO GOES with the TURTLE to the SEA Princess

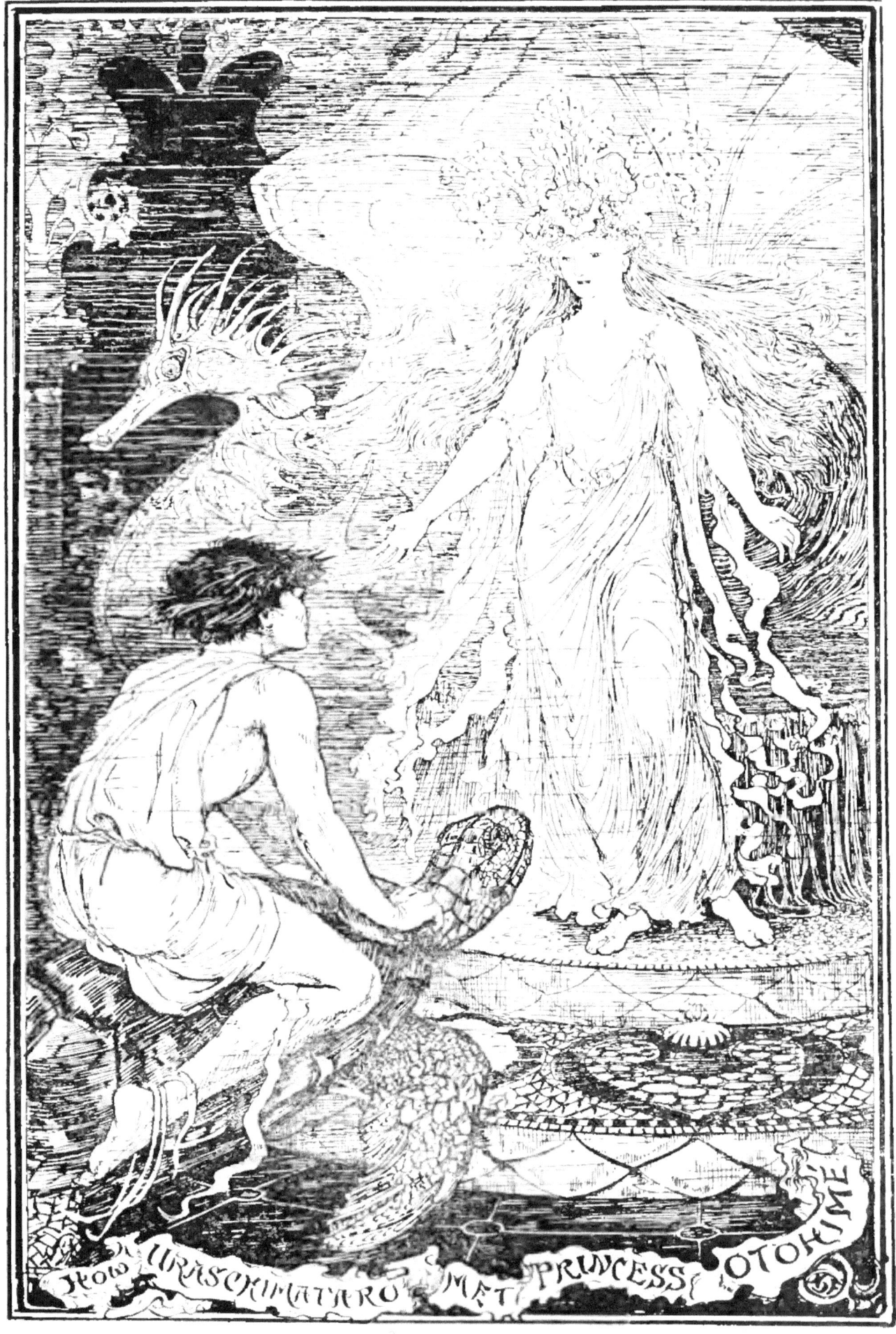

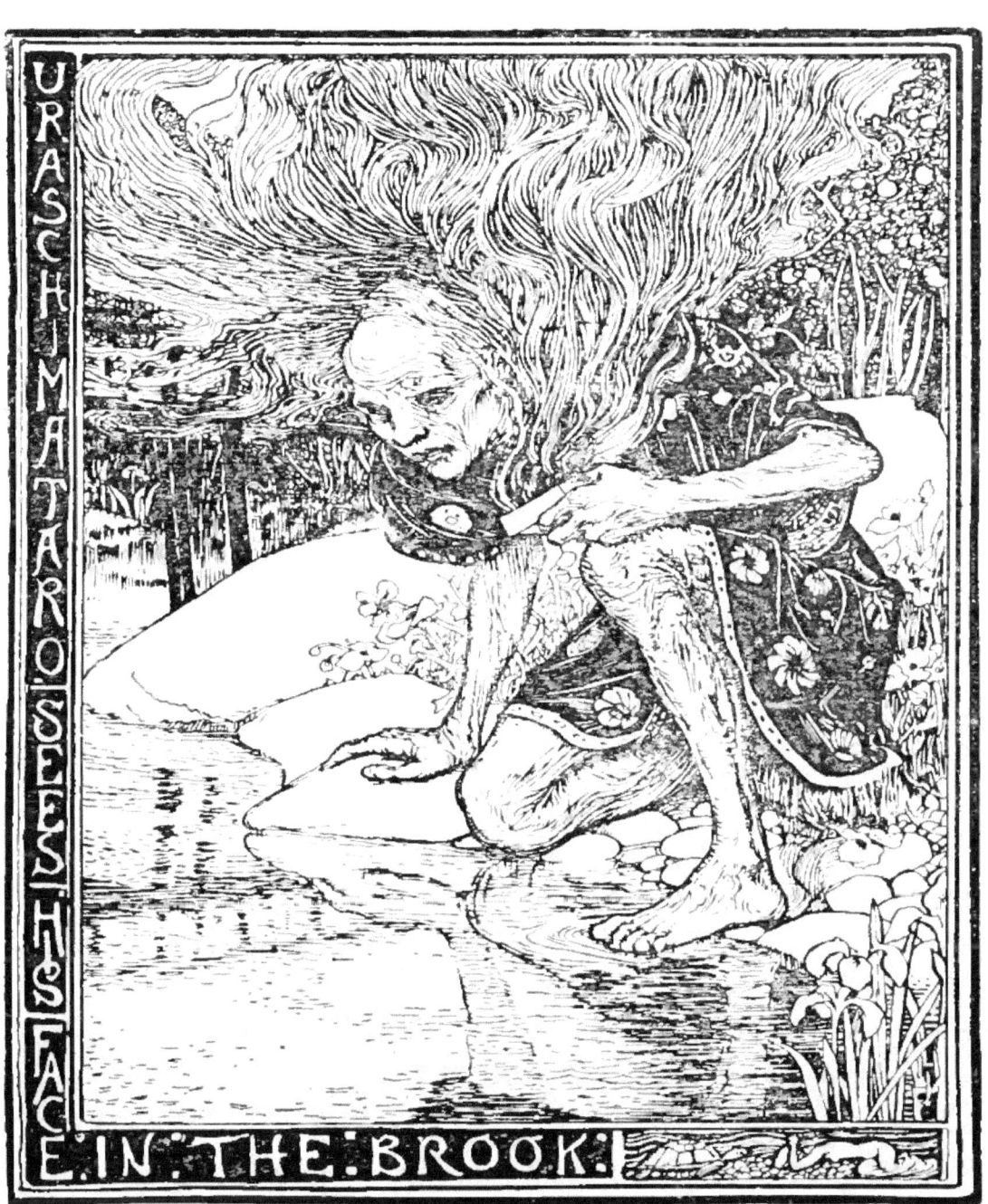

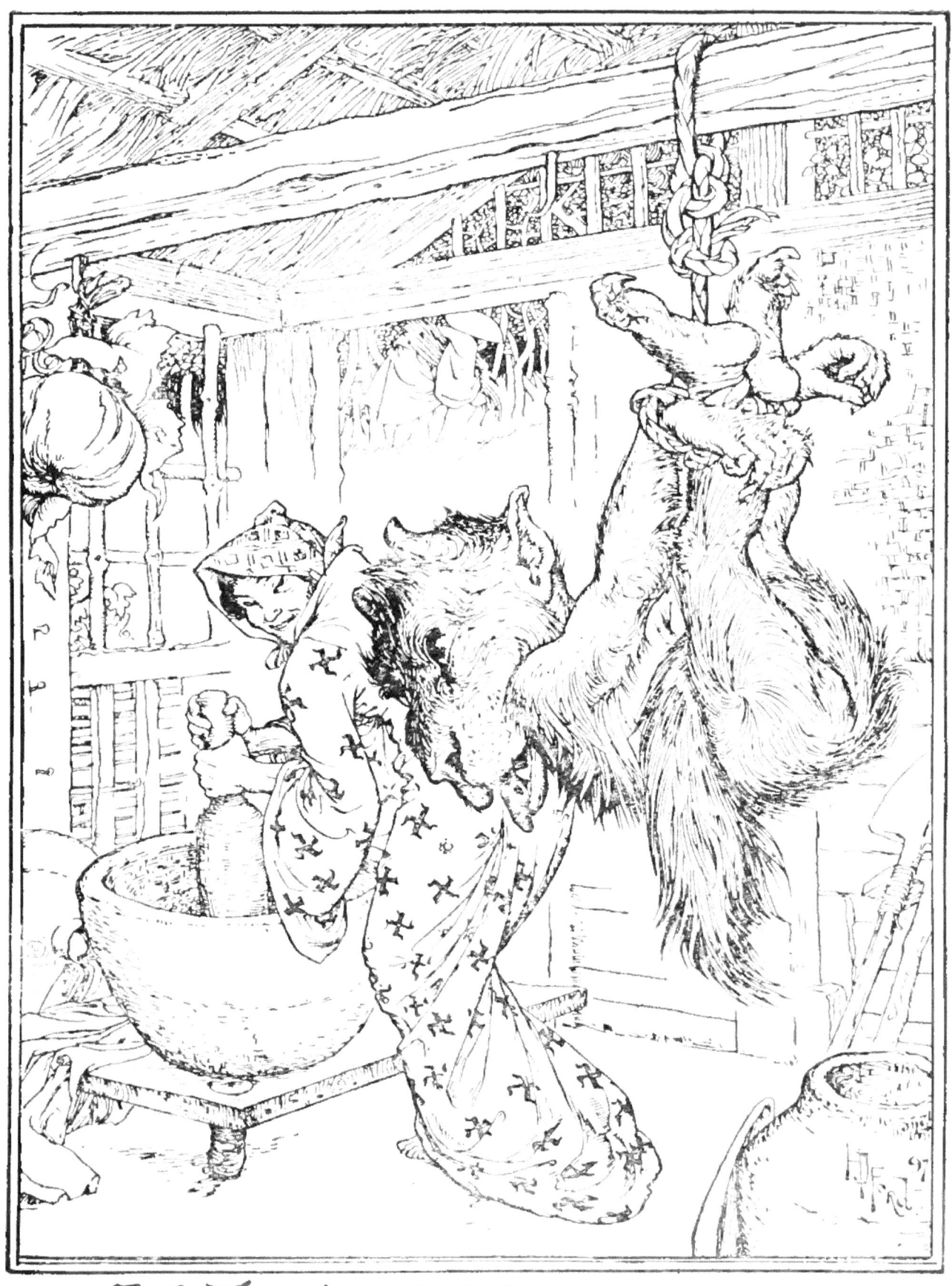

THE TANUKI BEGS THE OLD WOMAN TO RELEASE HIM

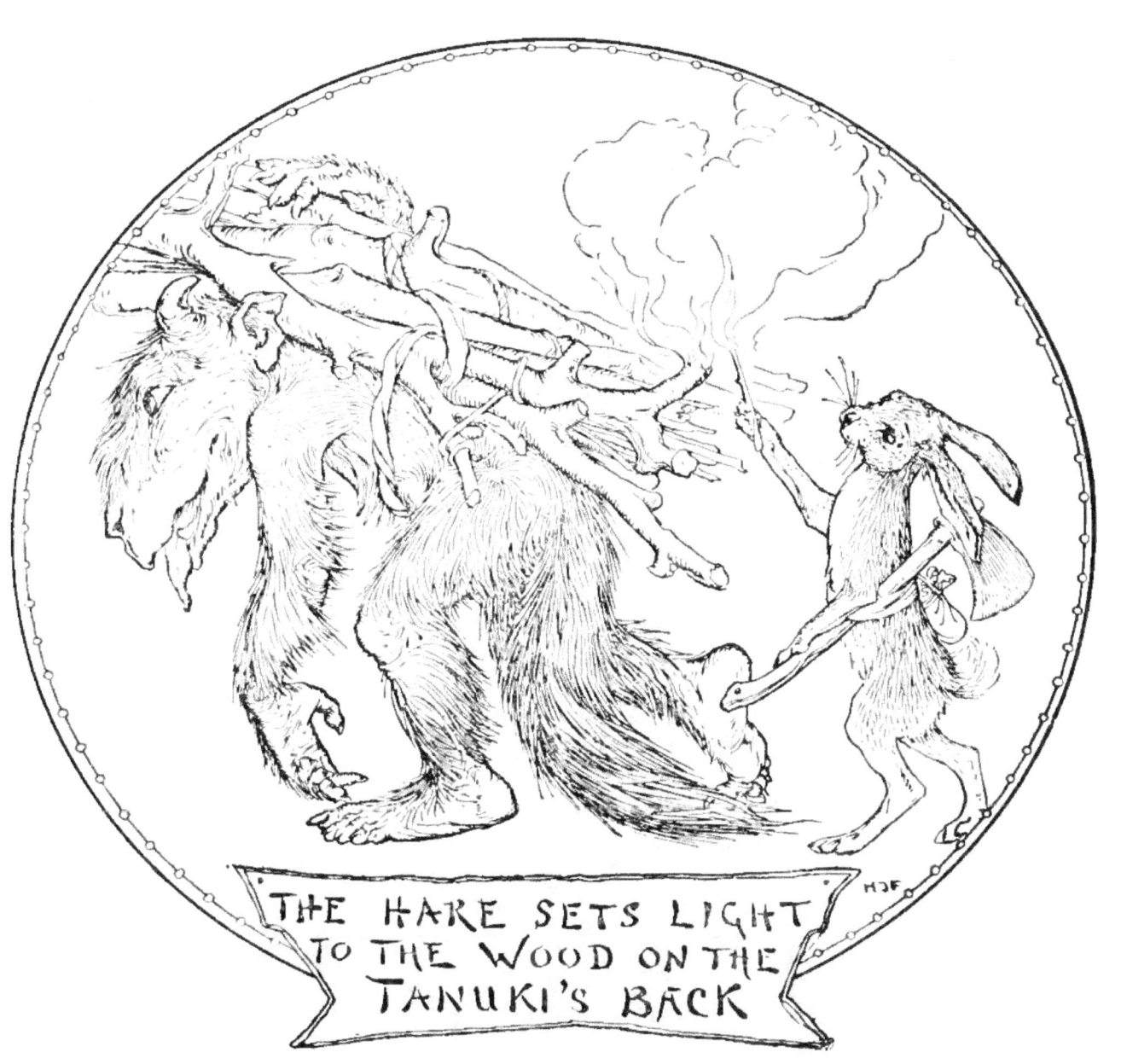

THE HARE SETS LIGHT TO THE WOOD ON THE TANUKI'S BACK

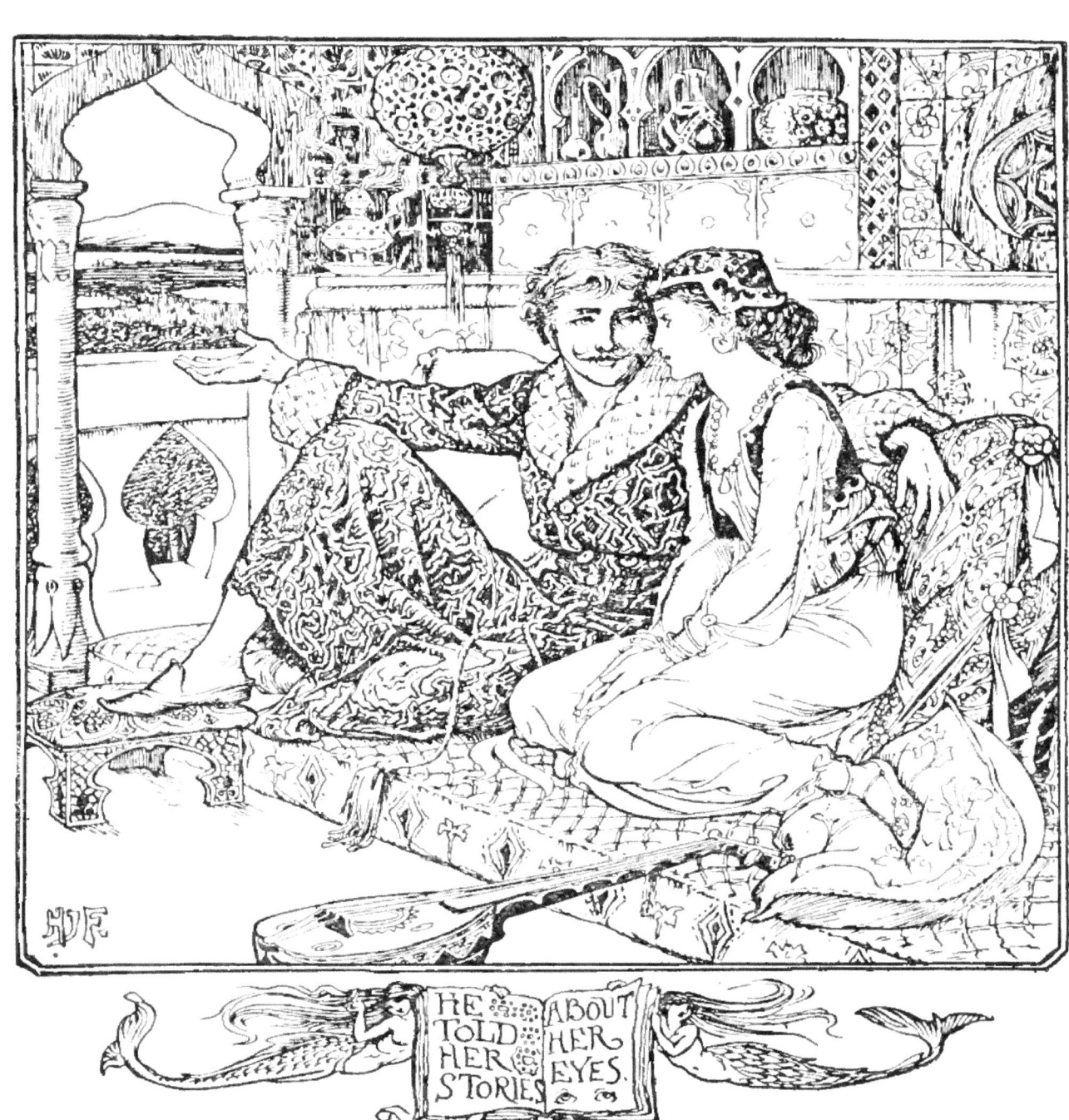

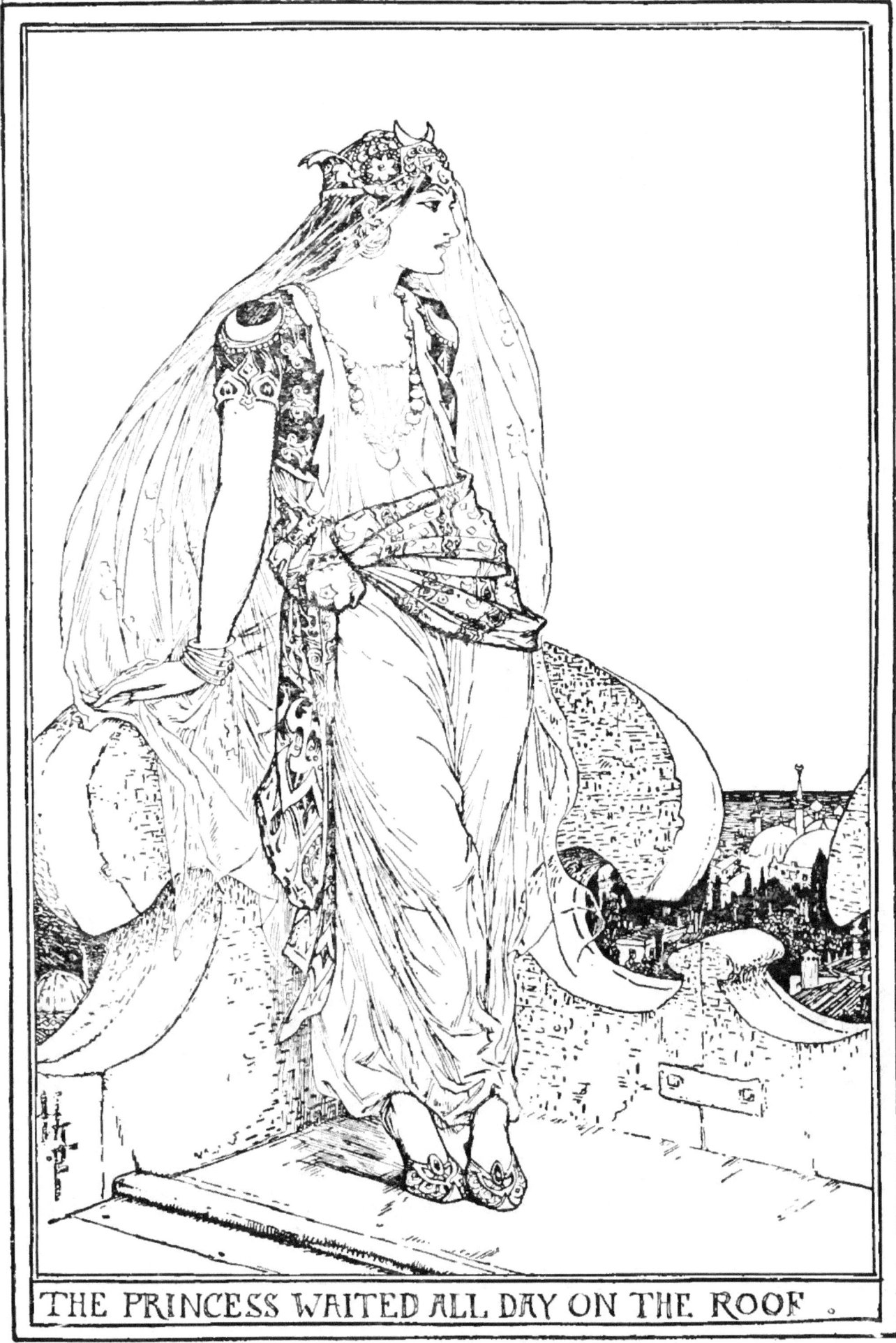

THE PRINCESS WAITED ALL DAY ON THE ROOF

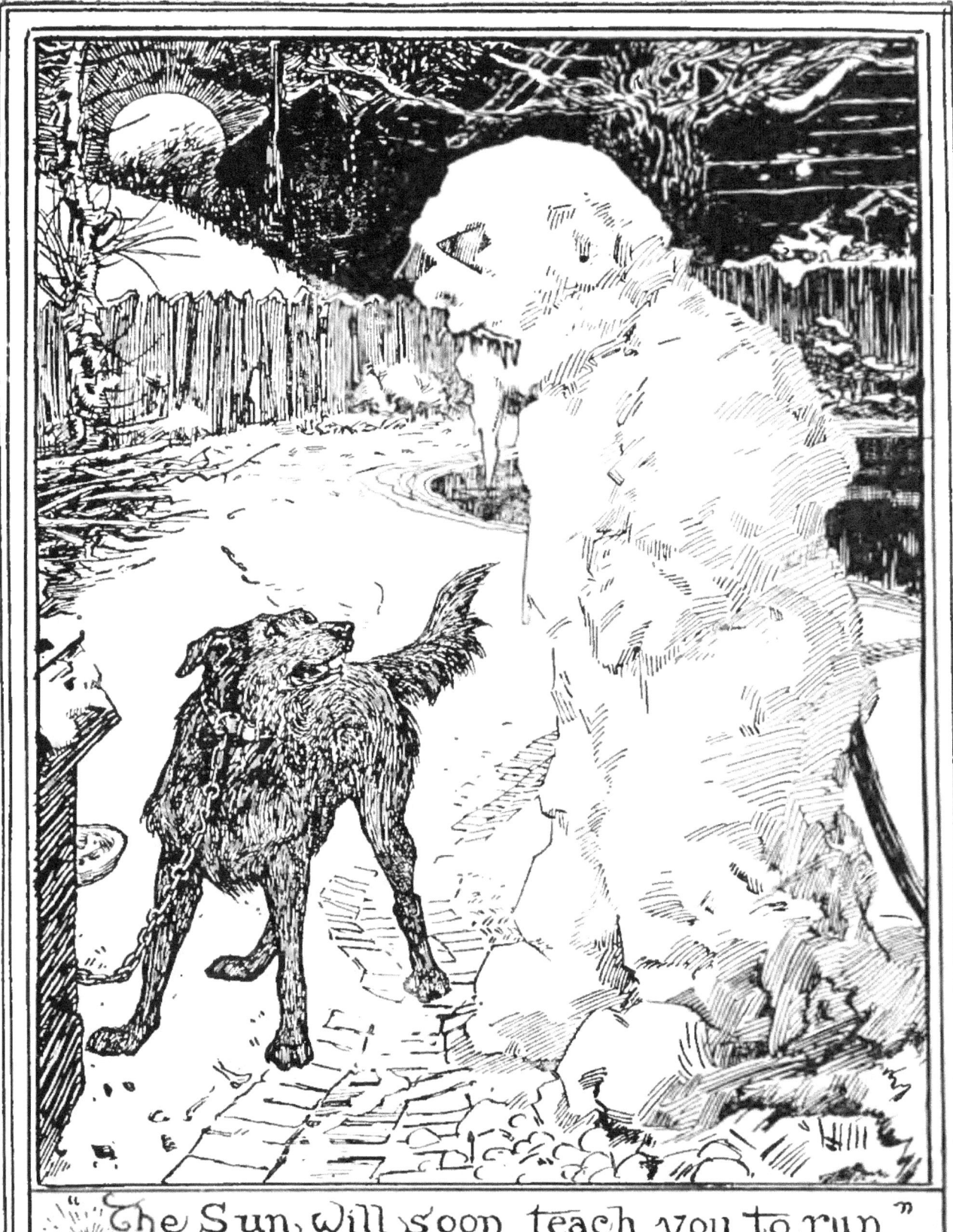

"The Sun will soon teach you to run" said the Yard-dog.

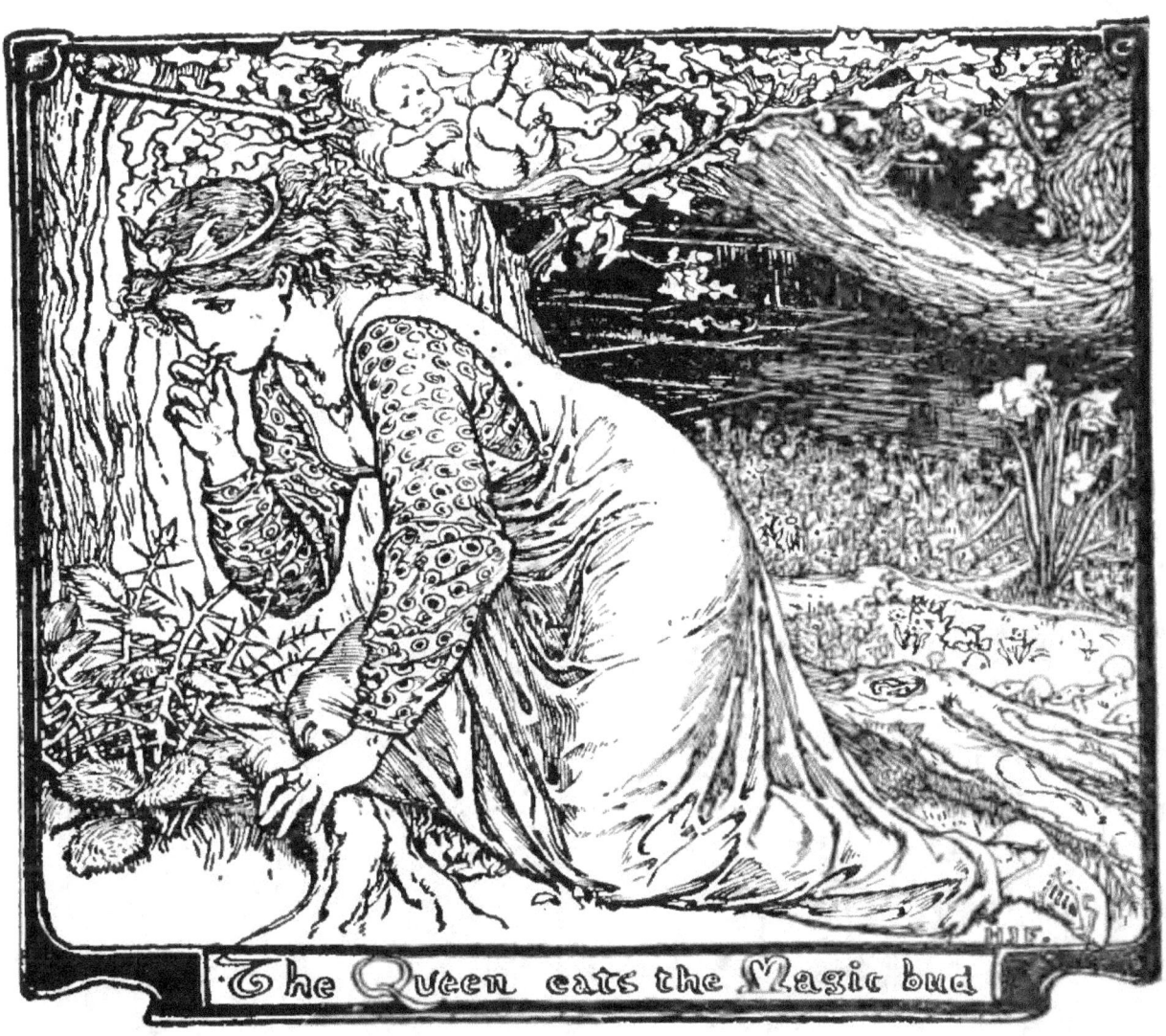

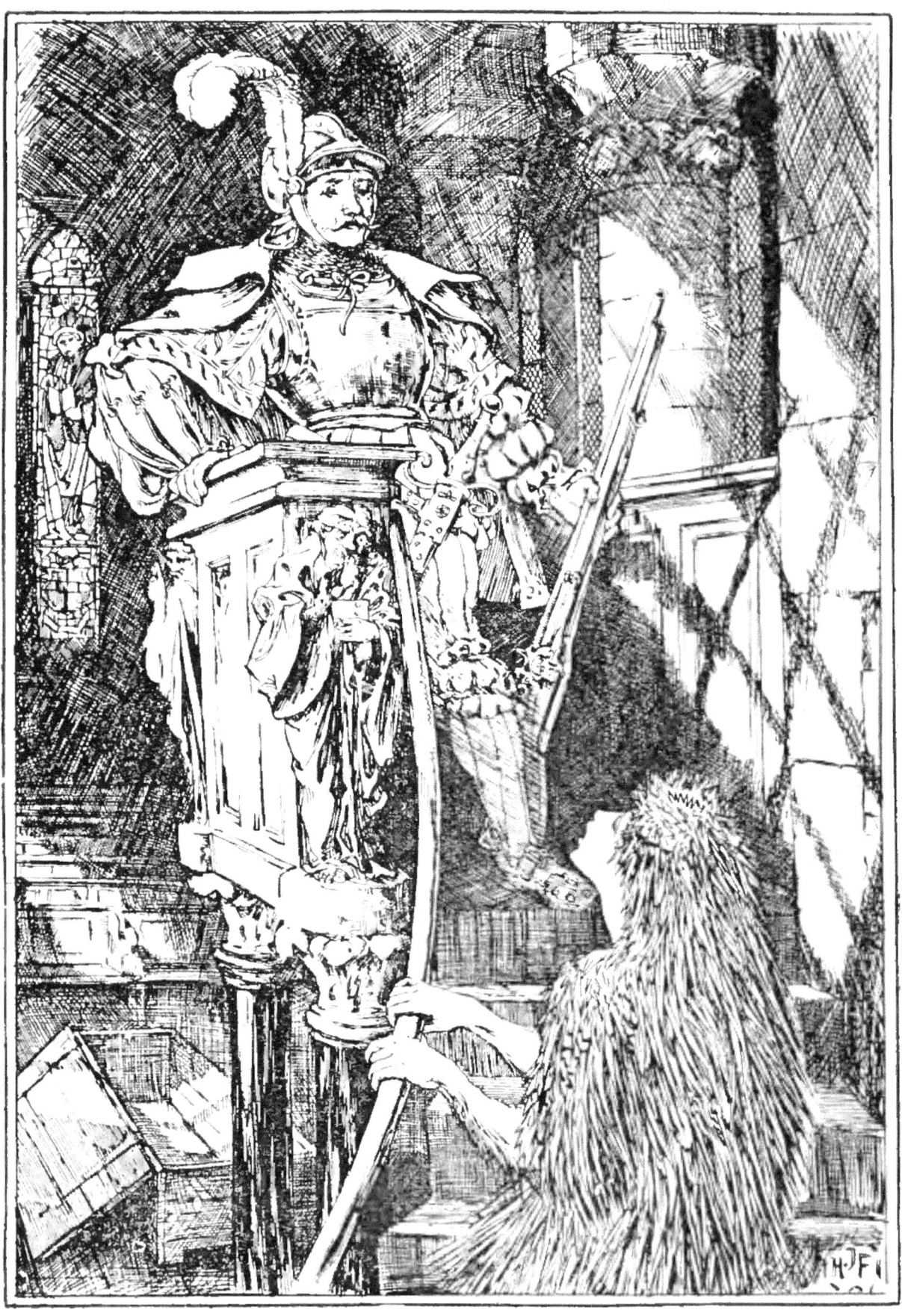

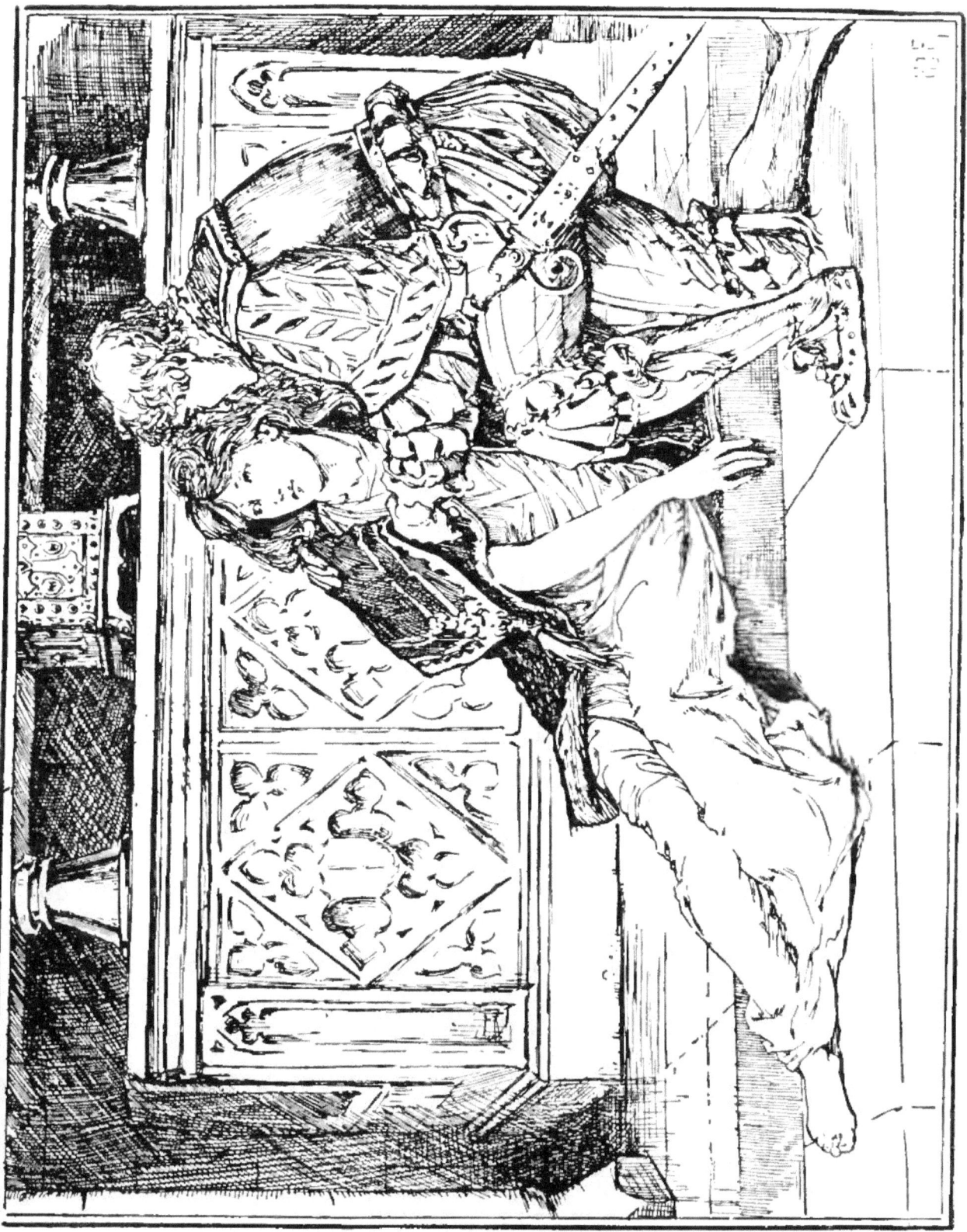

HE WRAPT HER IN HIS SOLDIER'S CLOAK.

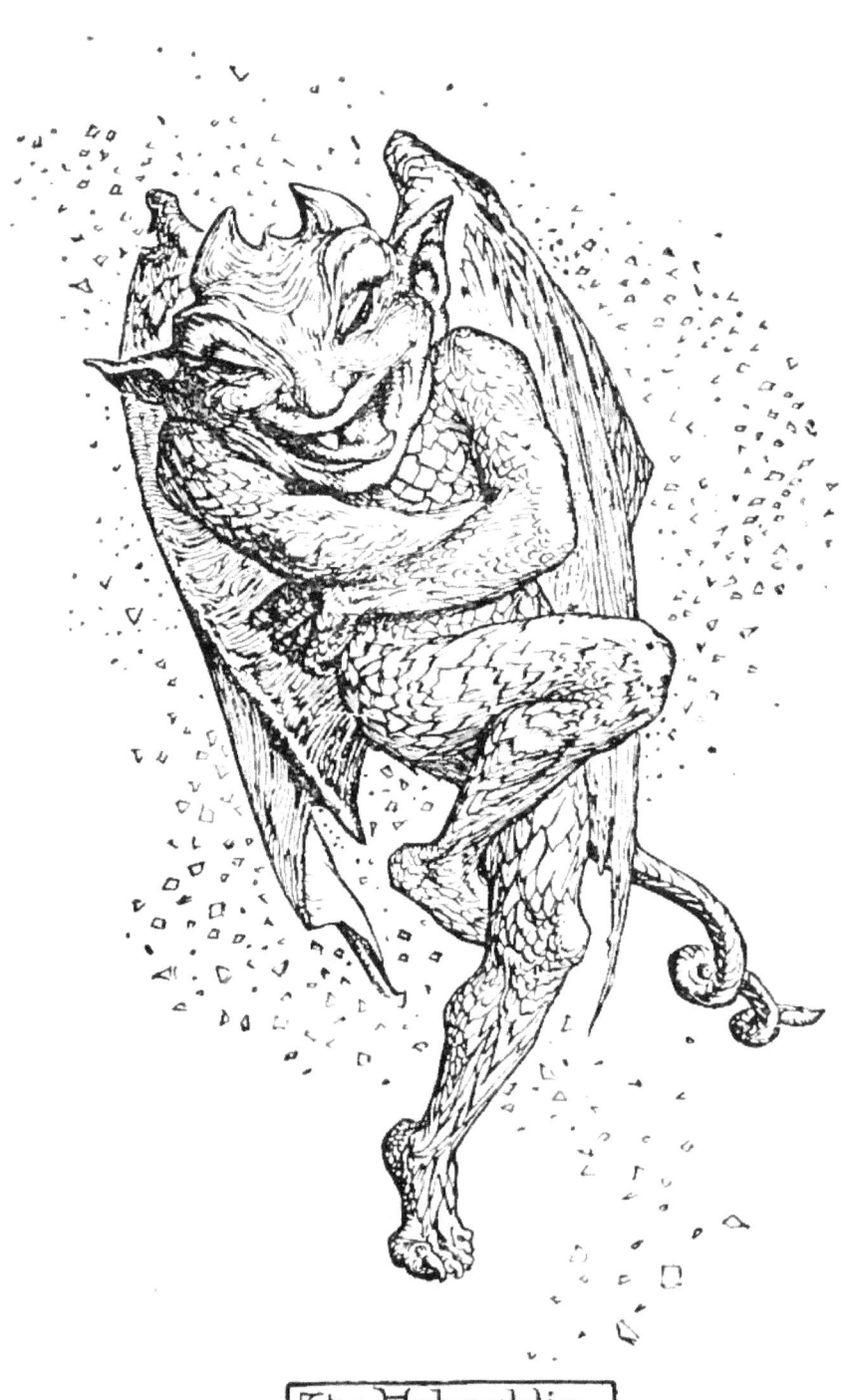

The Hobgoblin laughed till his sides ached

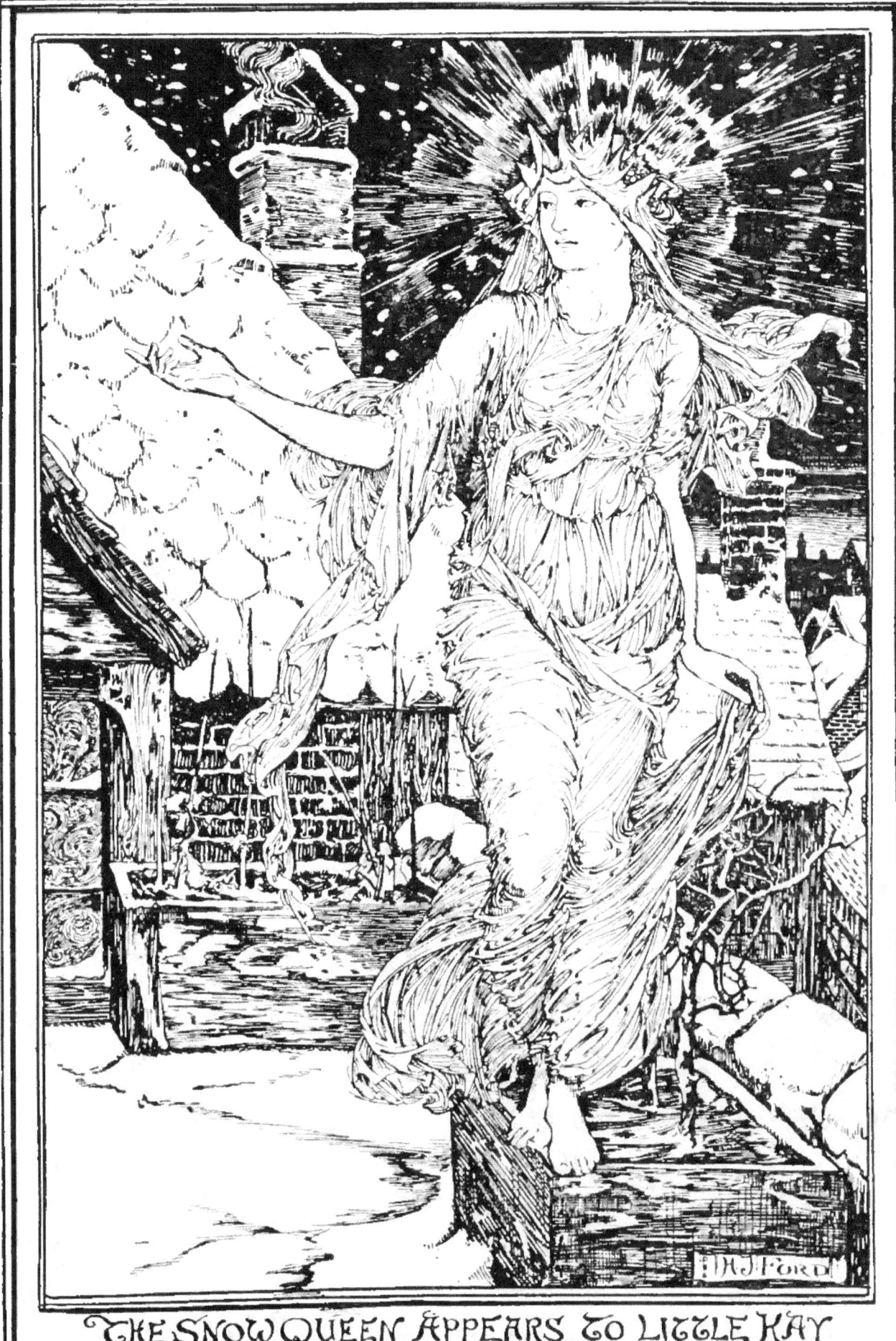
THE SNOW QUEEN APPEARS TO LITTLE KAY

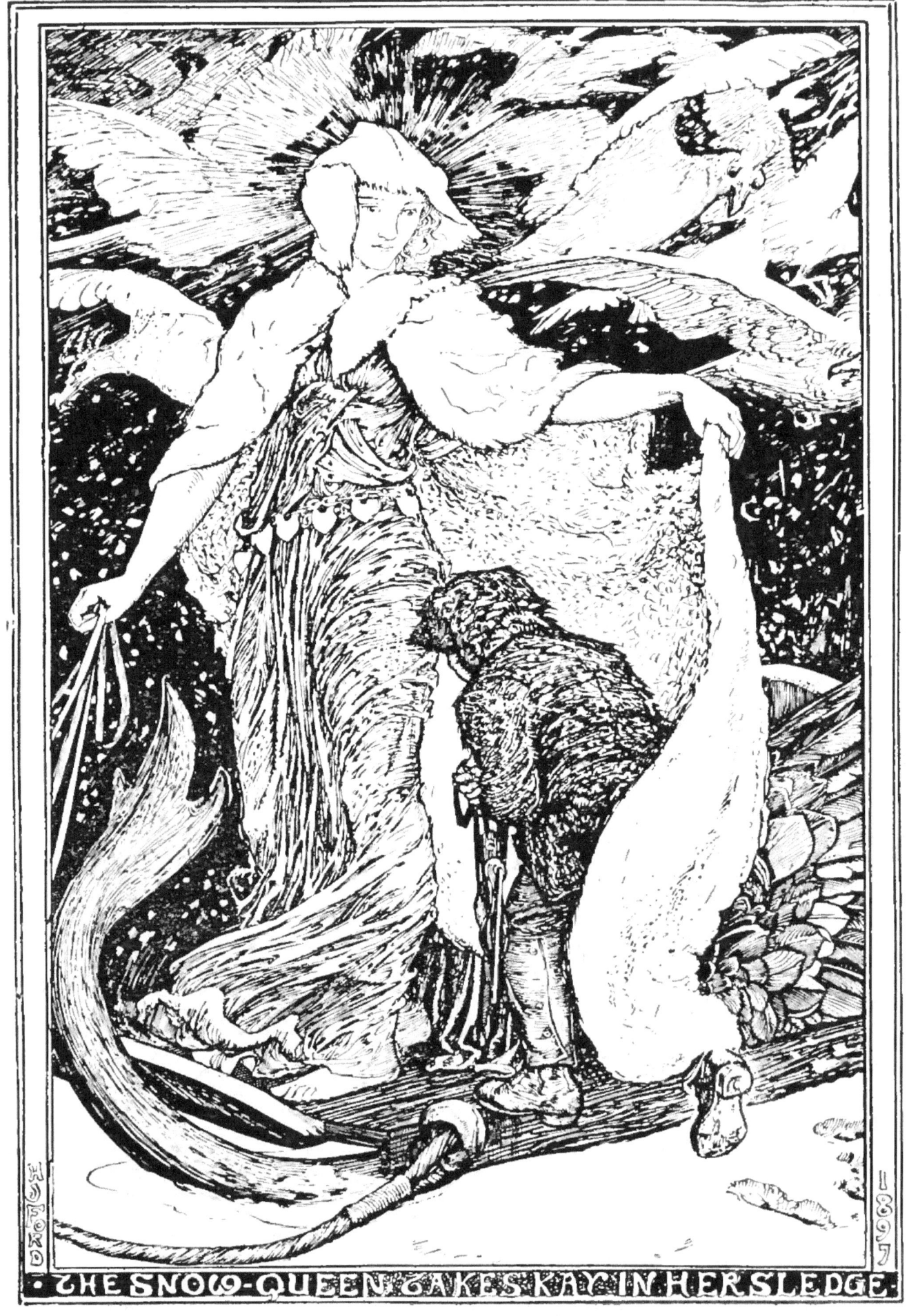
THE SNOW-QUEEN TAKES KAY IN HER SLEDGE

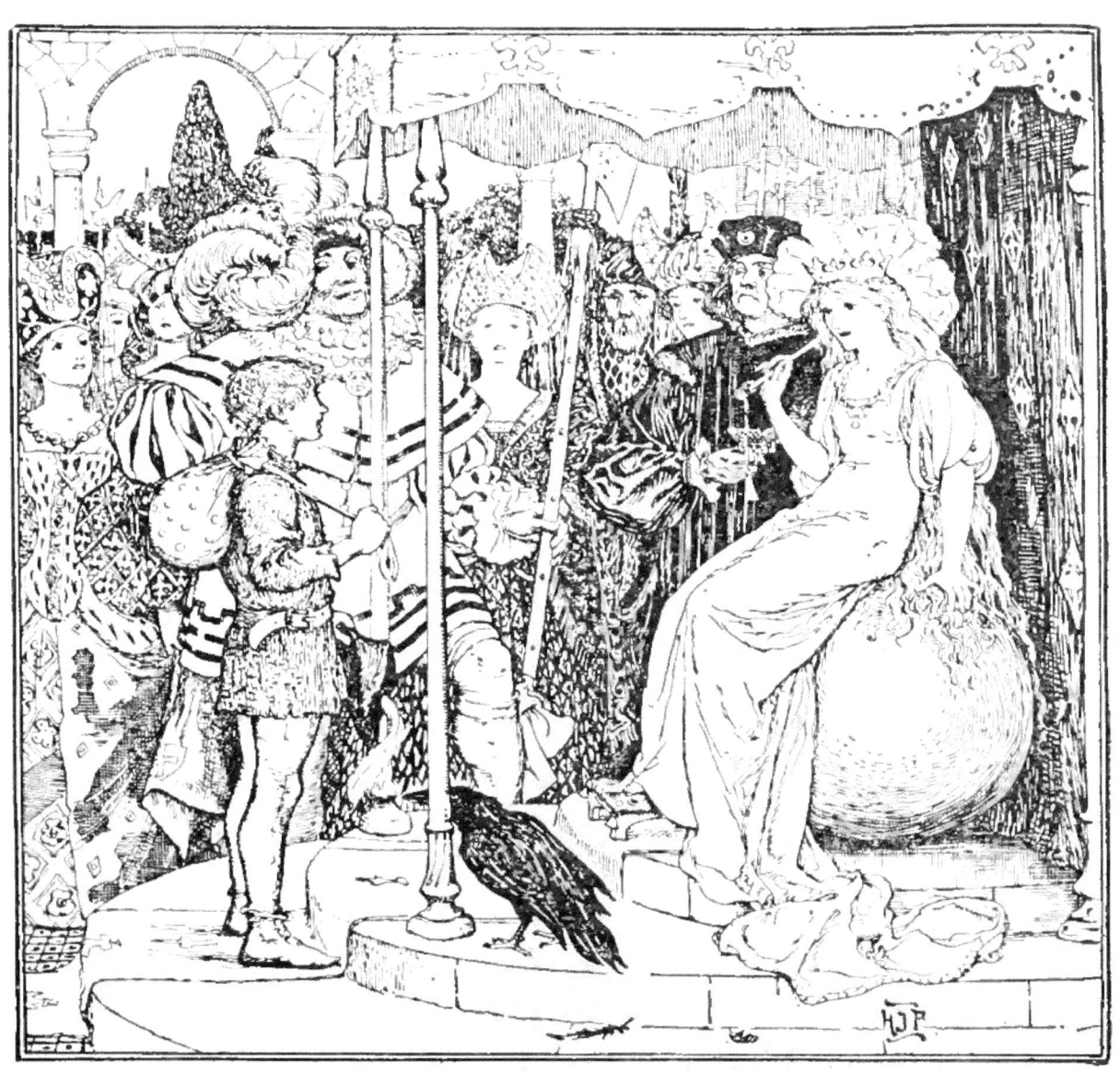

'HE HAD NOT COME TO WOO' HE SAID

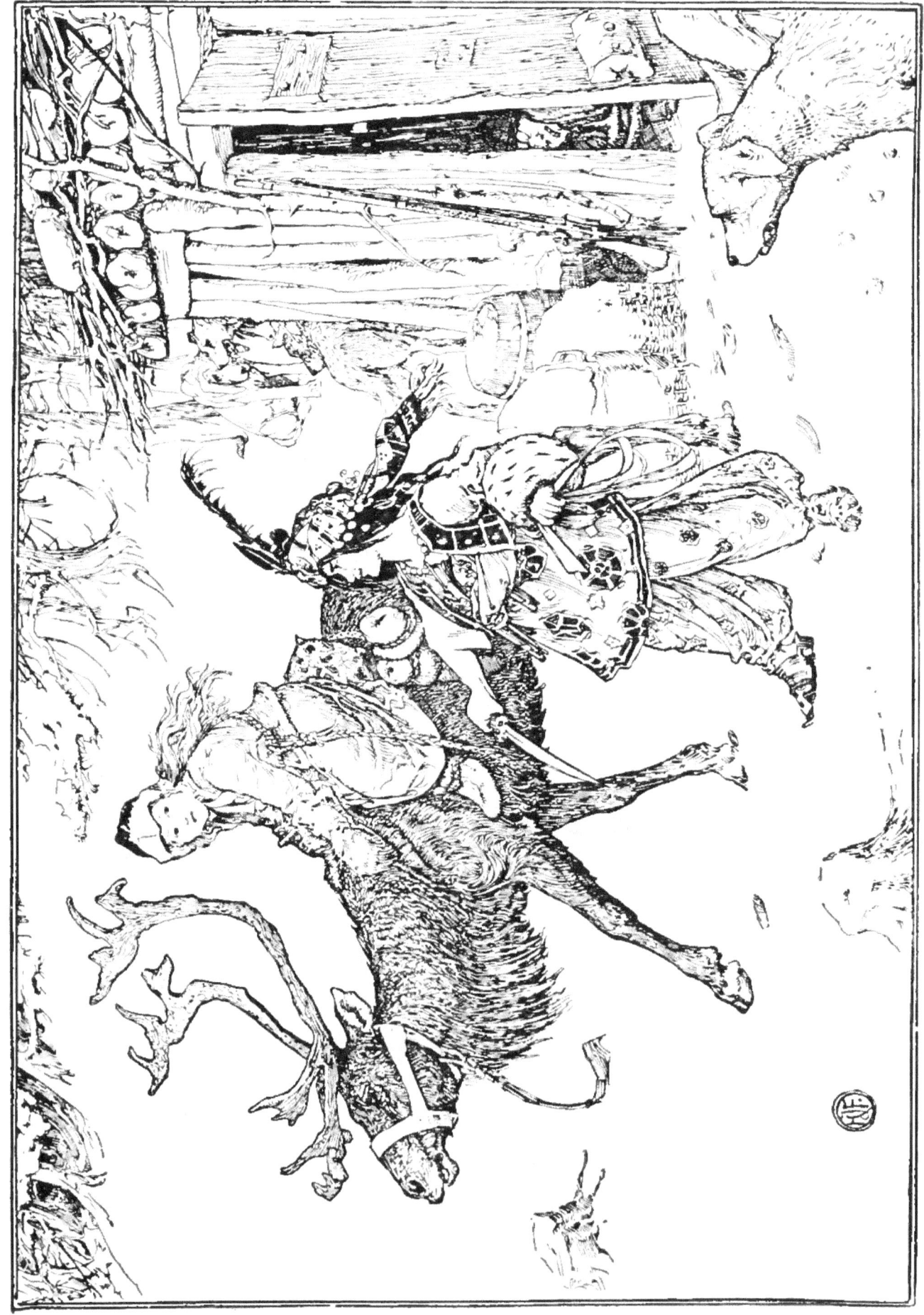

The Robber-girl sends Gerda off on the Reindeer.

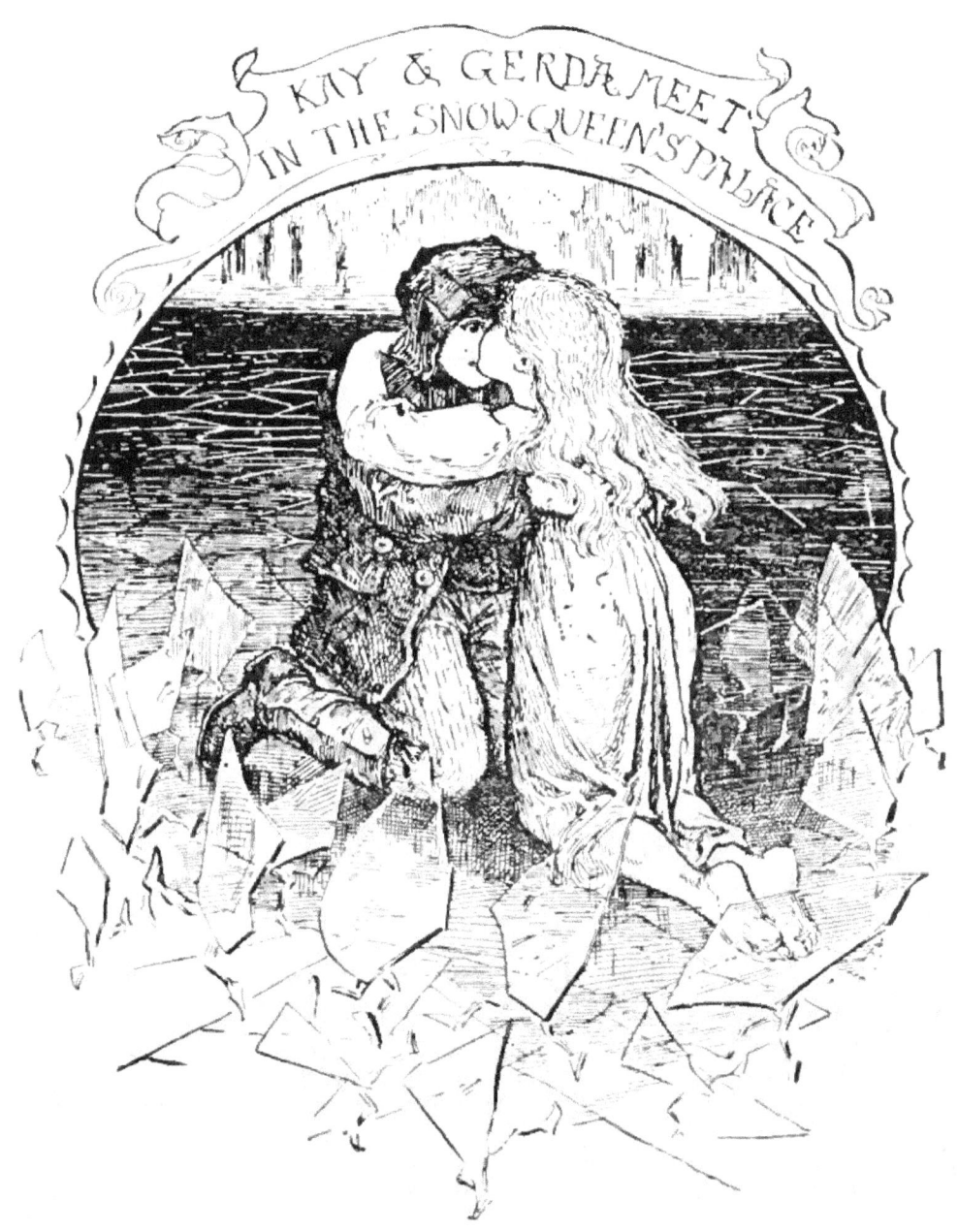

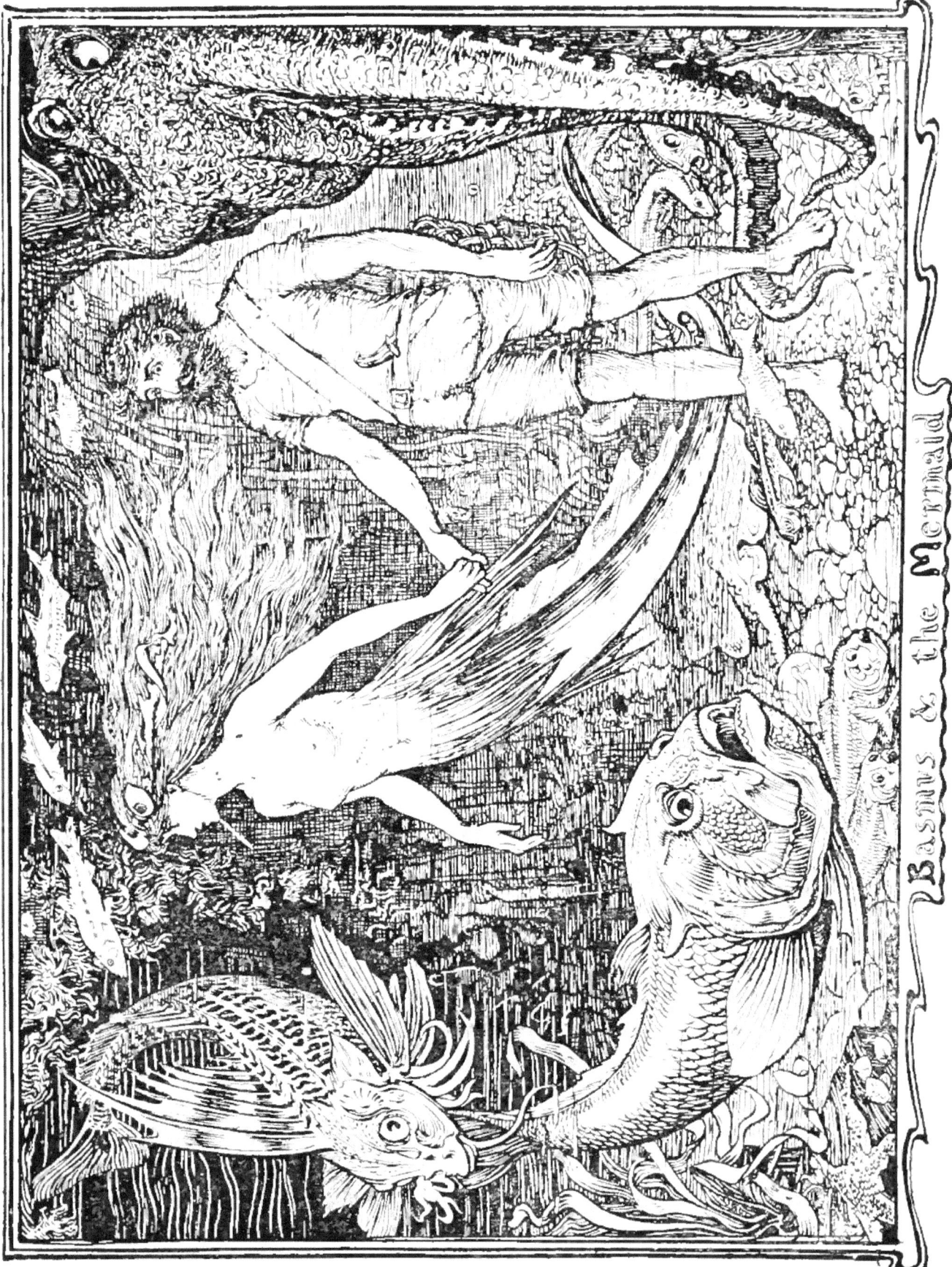

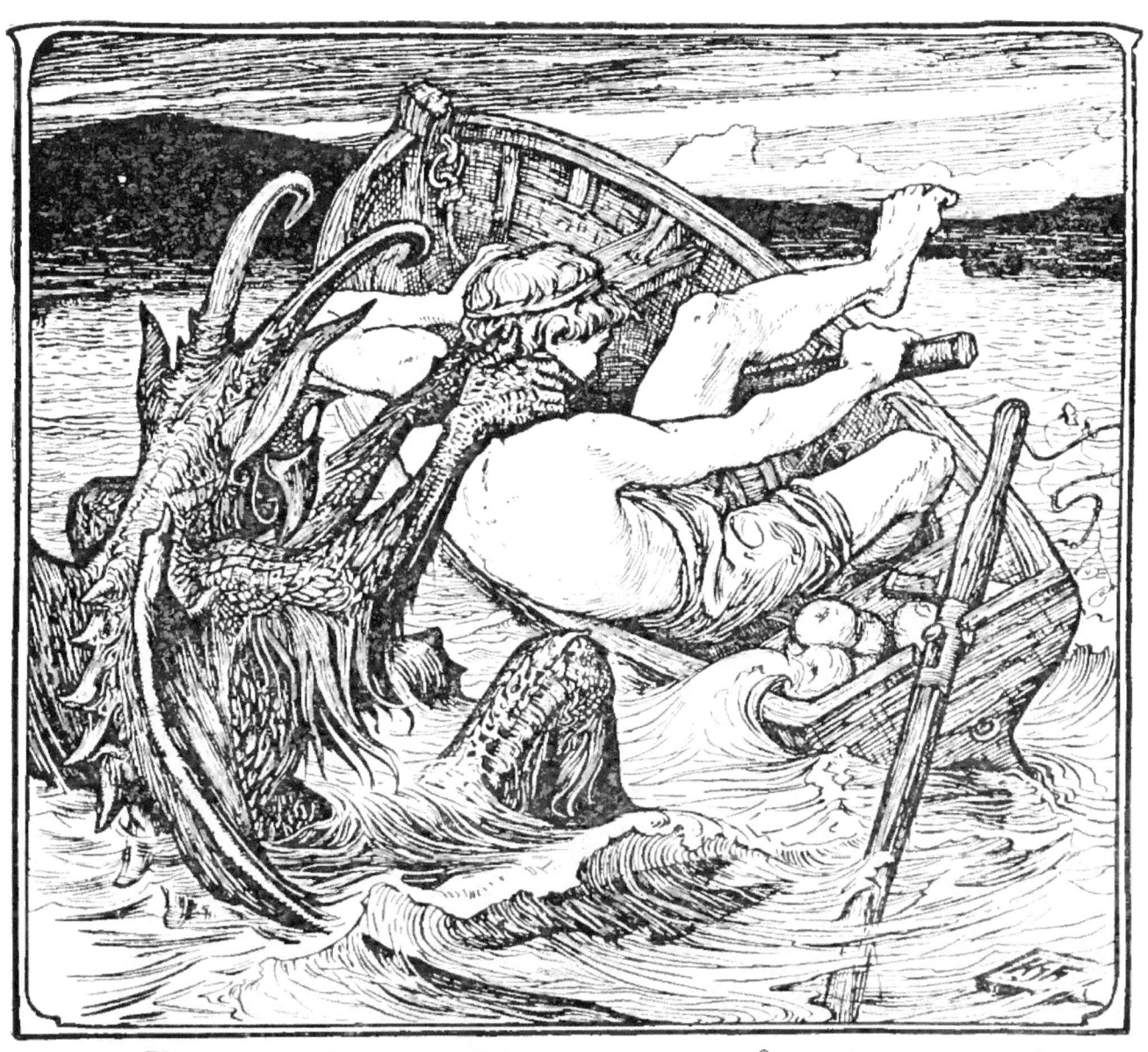

OLD ERIC CATCHES HANS

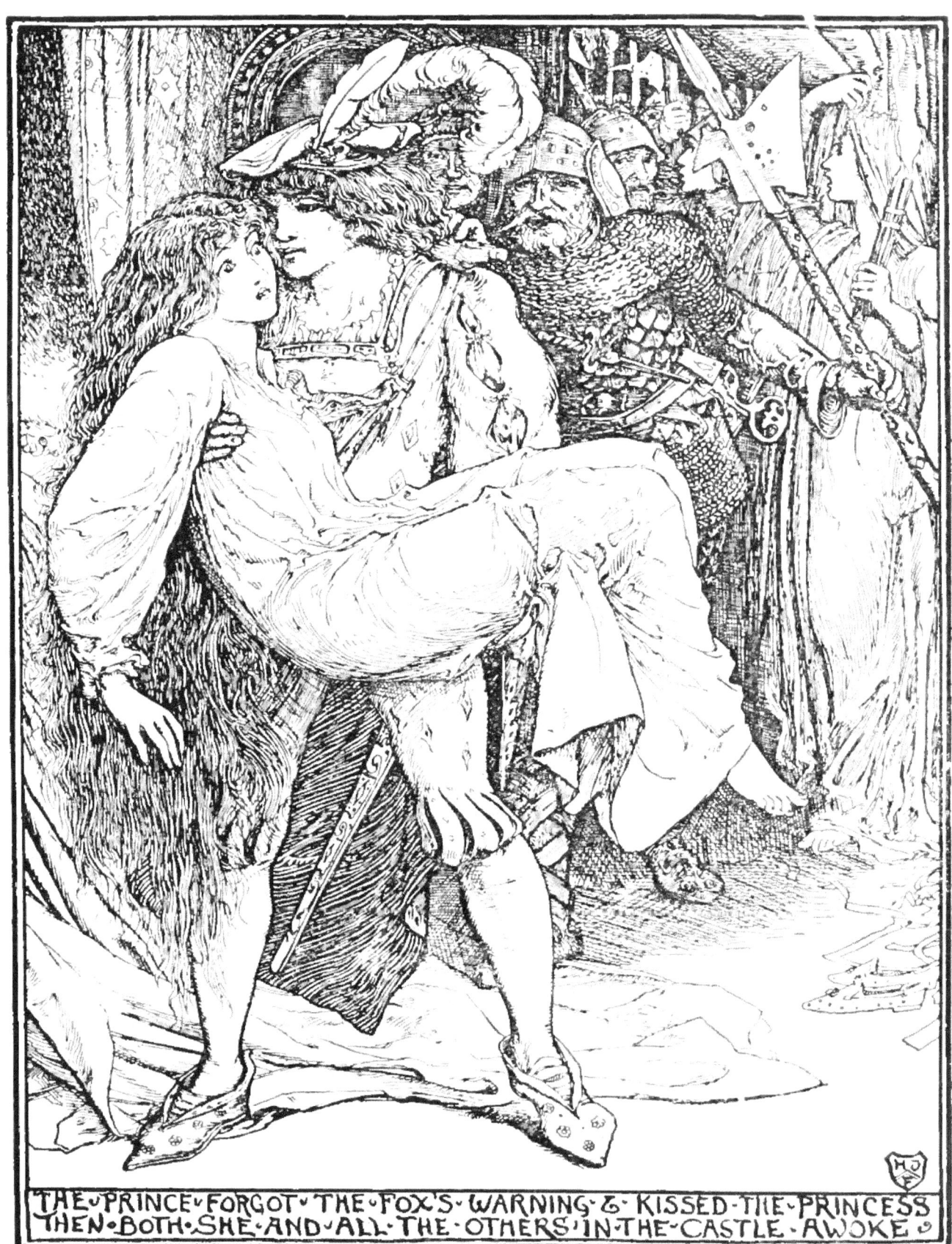

THE PRINCE FORGOT THE FOX'S WARNING & KISSED THE PRINCESS THEN BOTH SHE AND ALL THE OTHERS IN THE CASTLE AWOKE

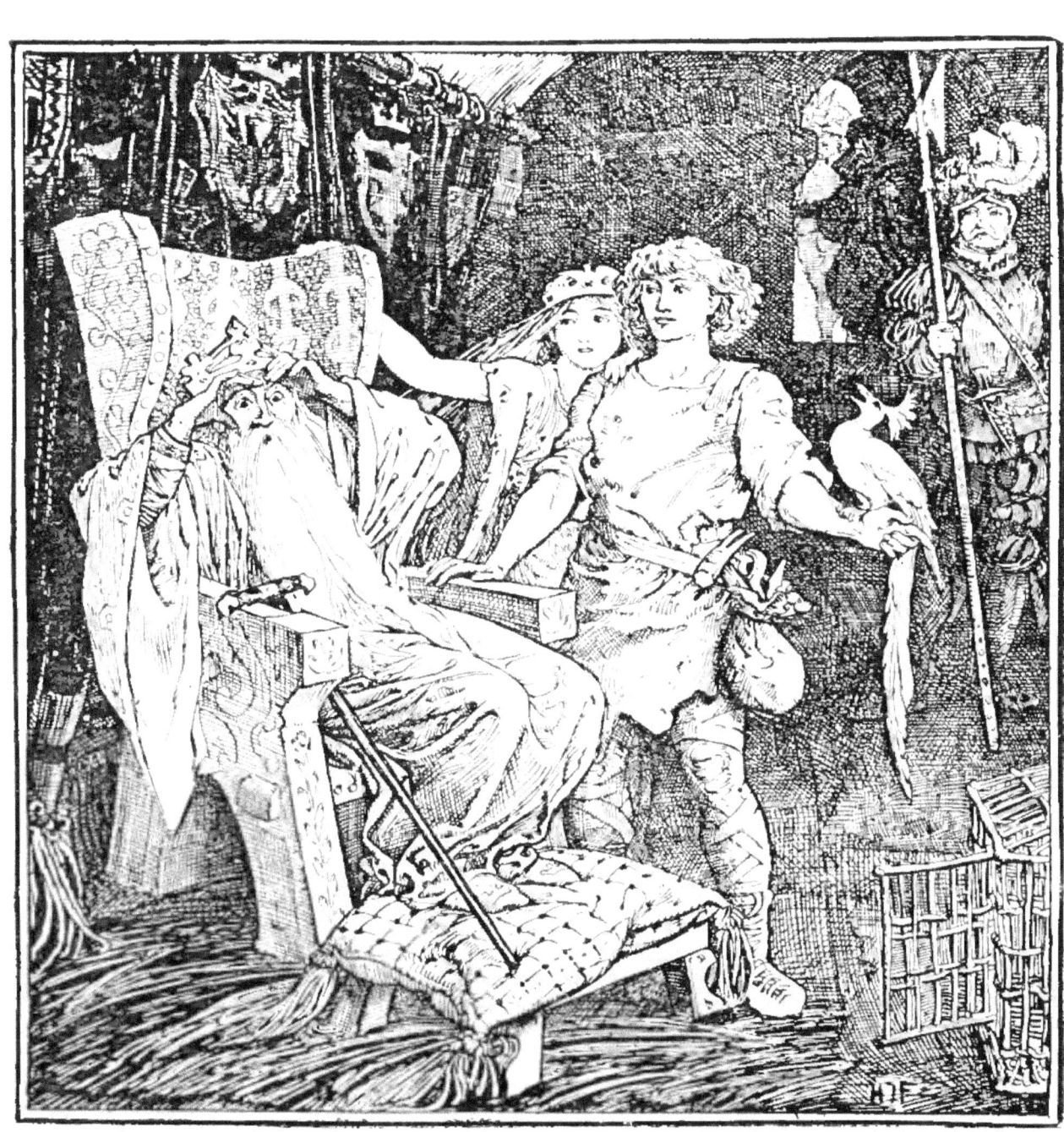

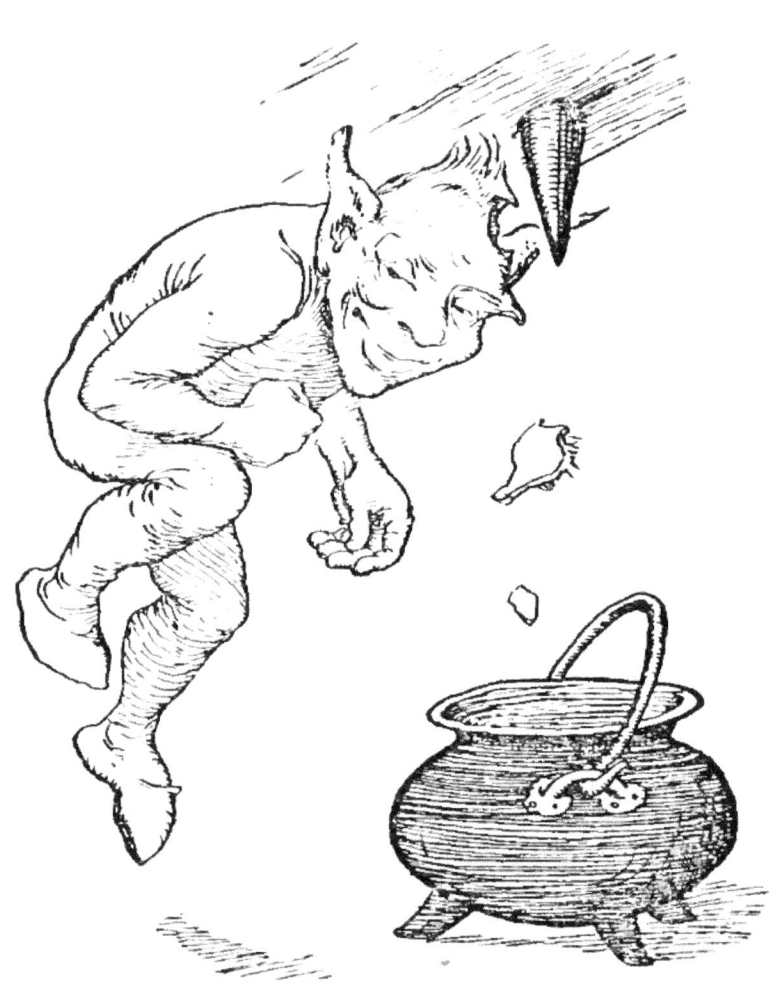

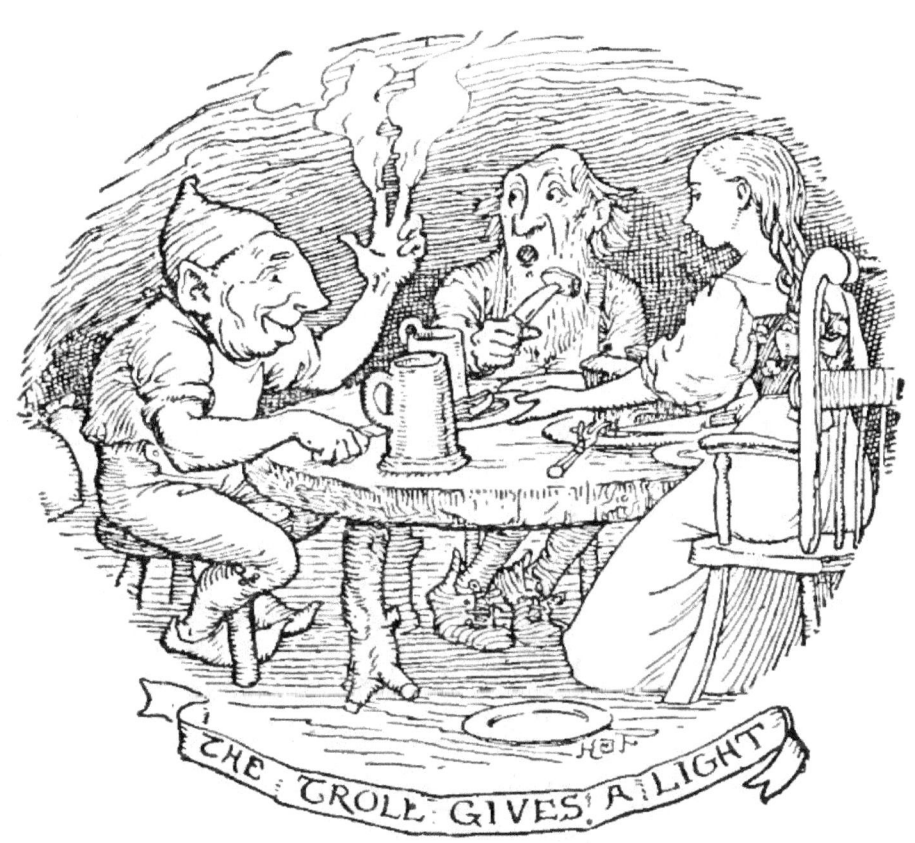

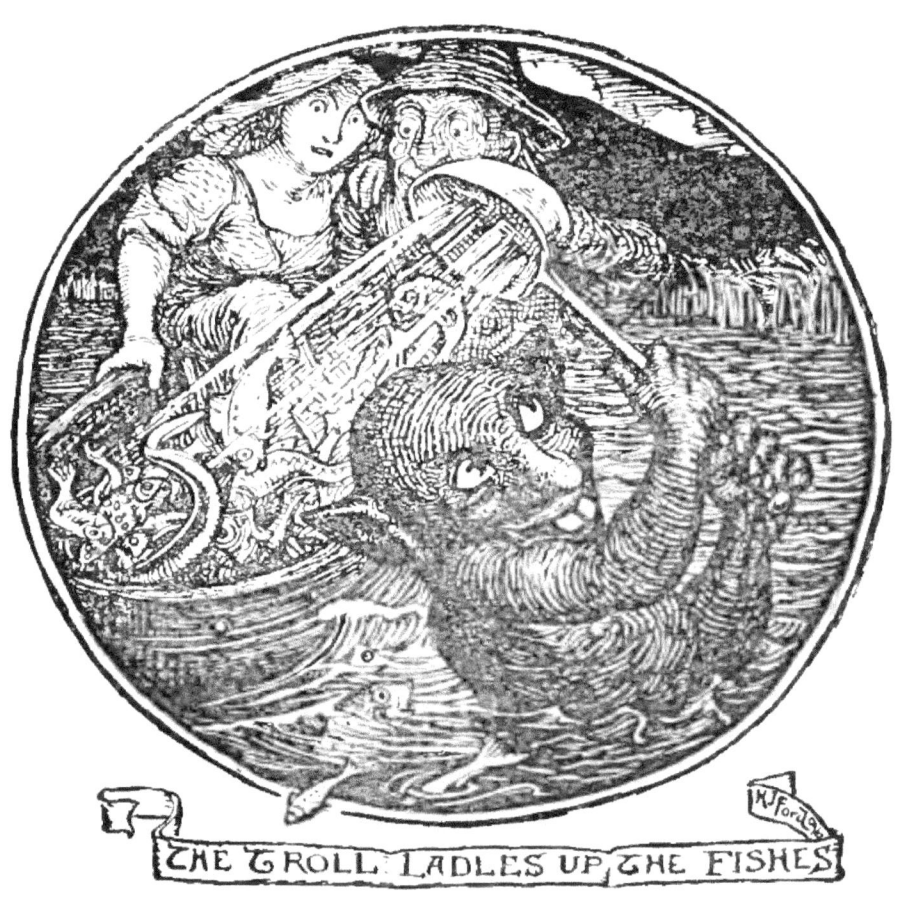

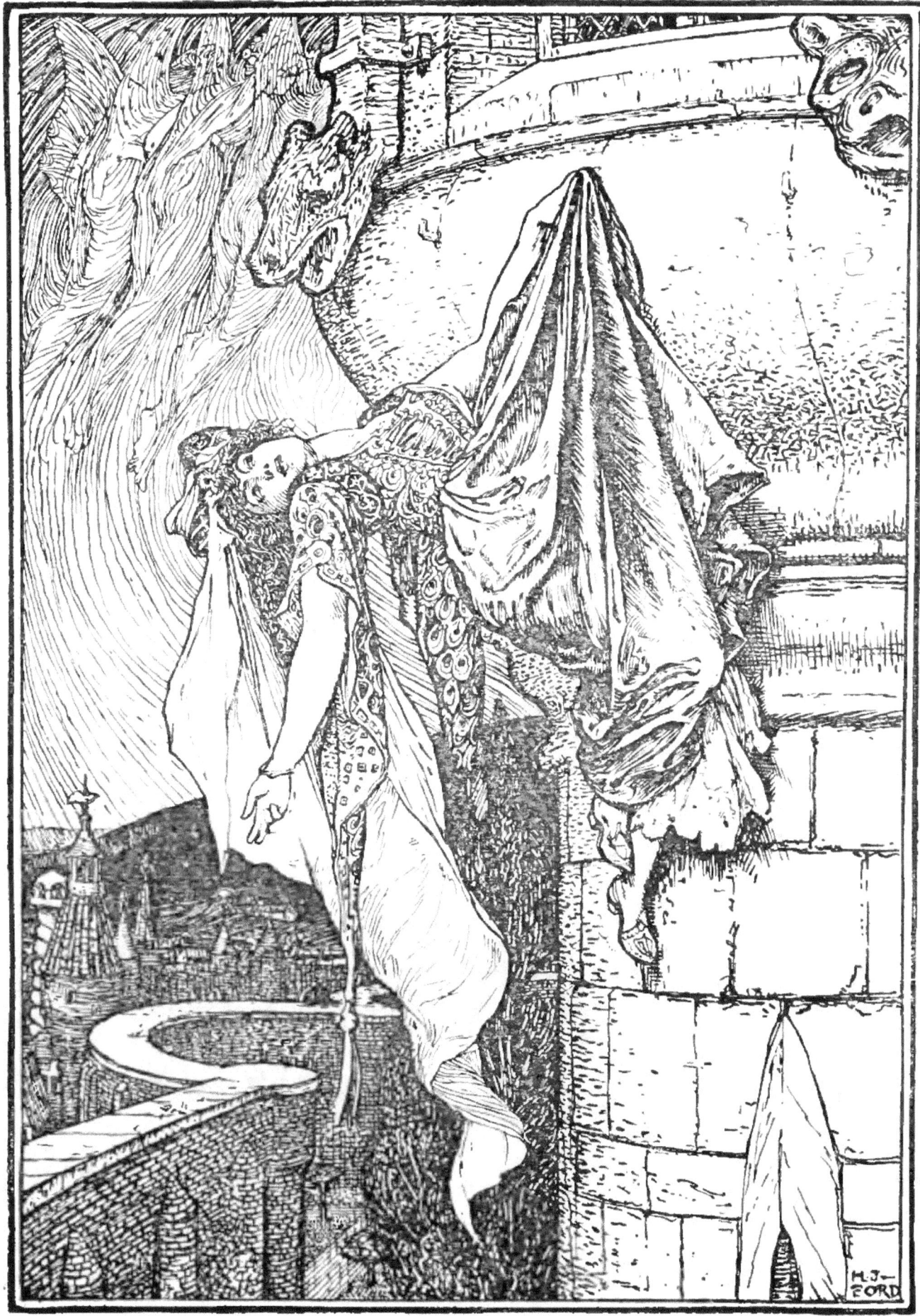

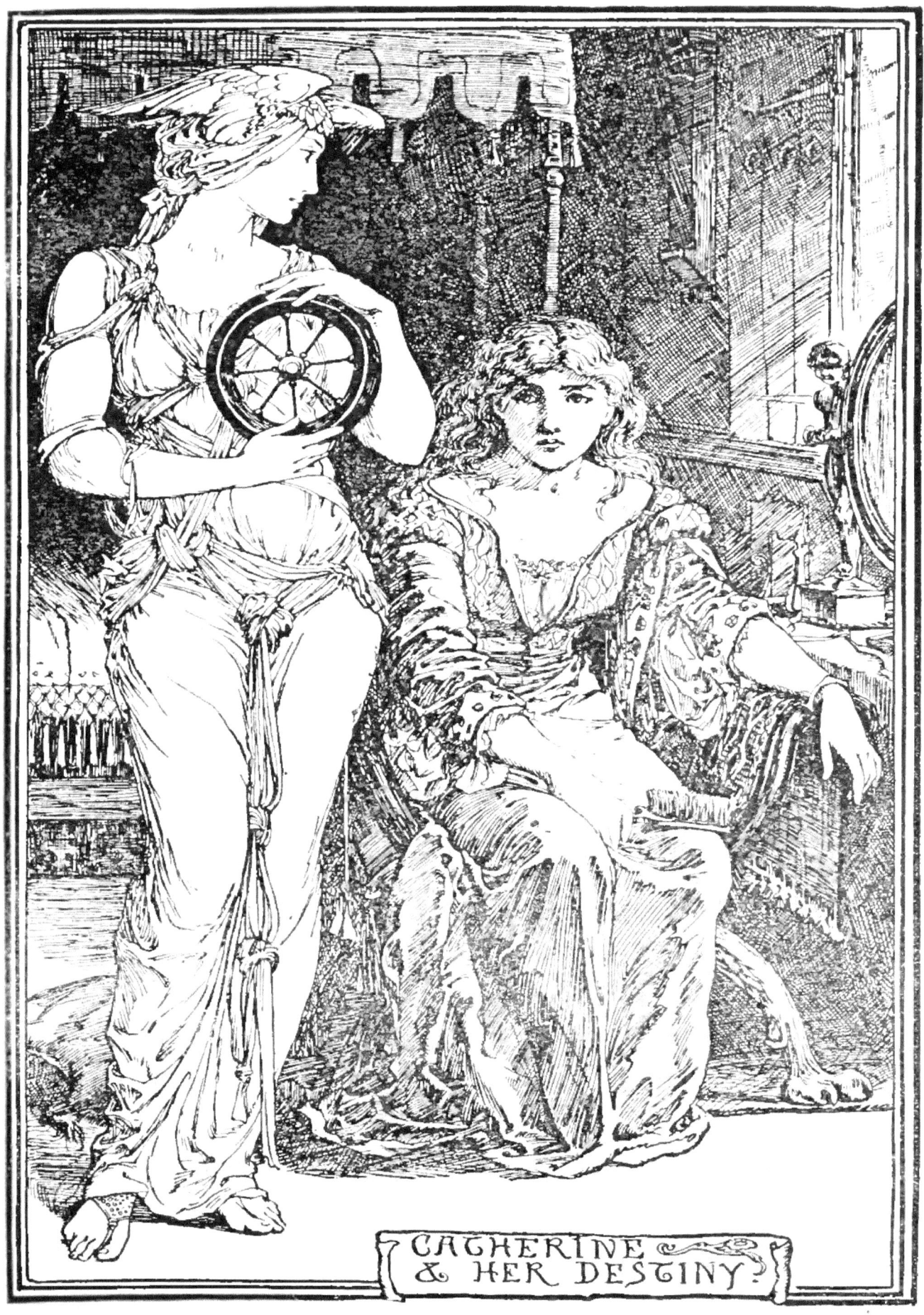

CATHERINE & HER DESTINY.

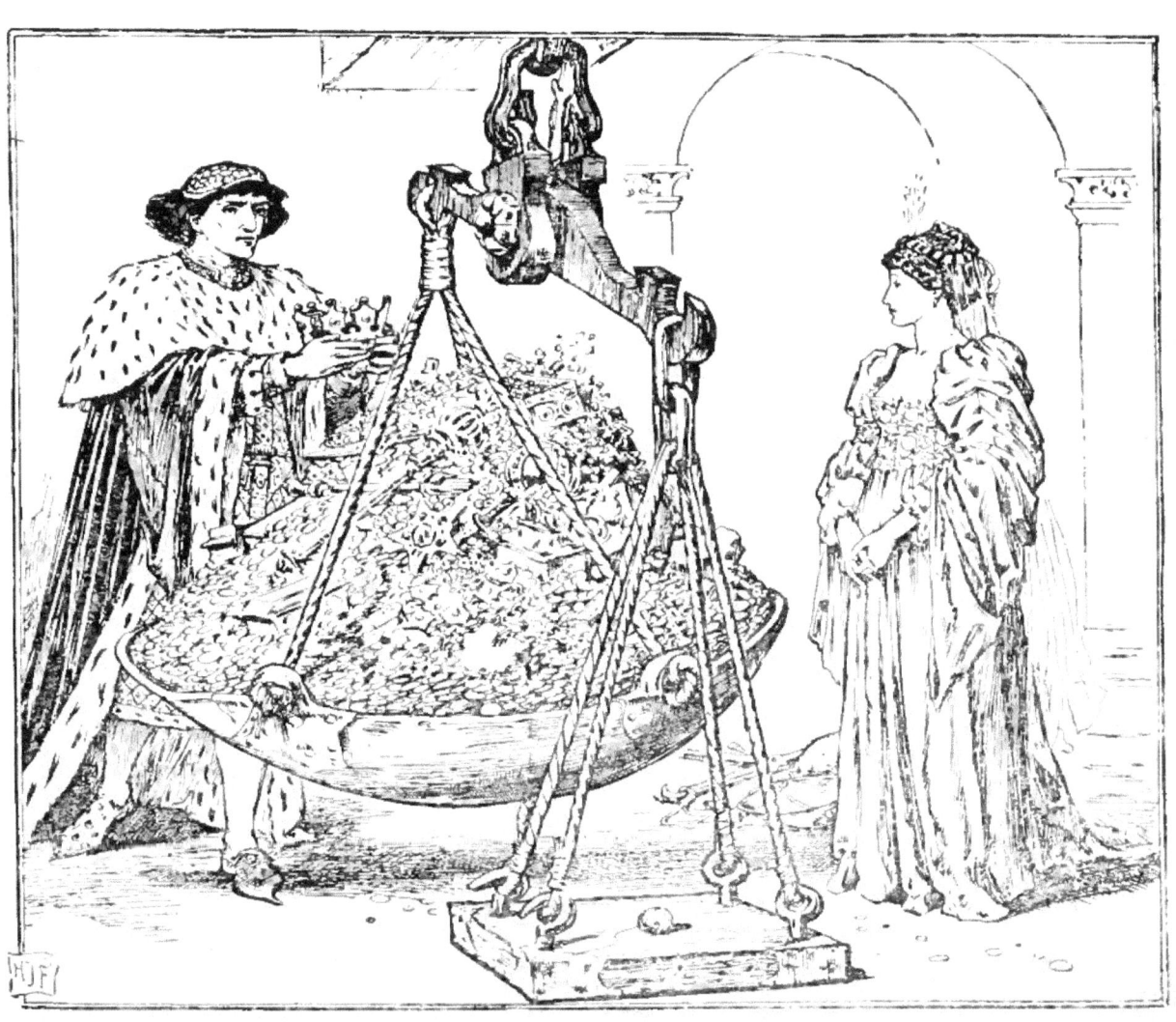

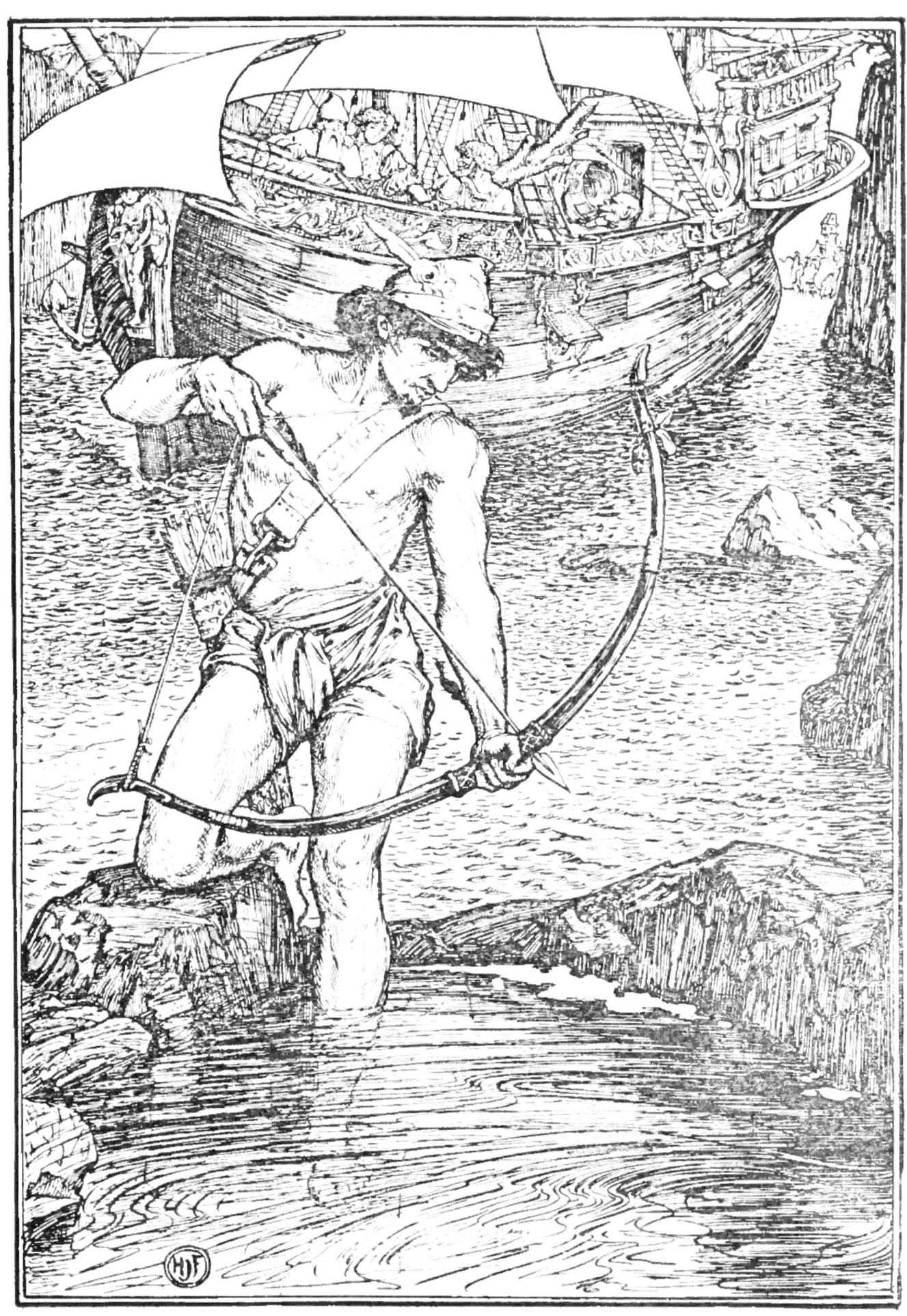

HOW THEY MET THE ARCHER IN THE STREAM.

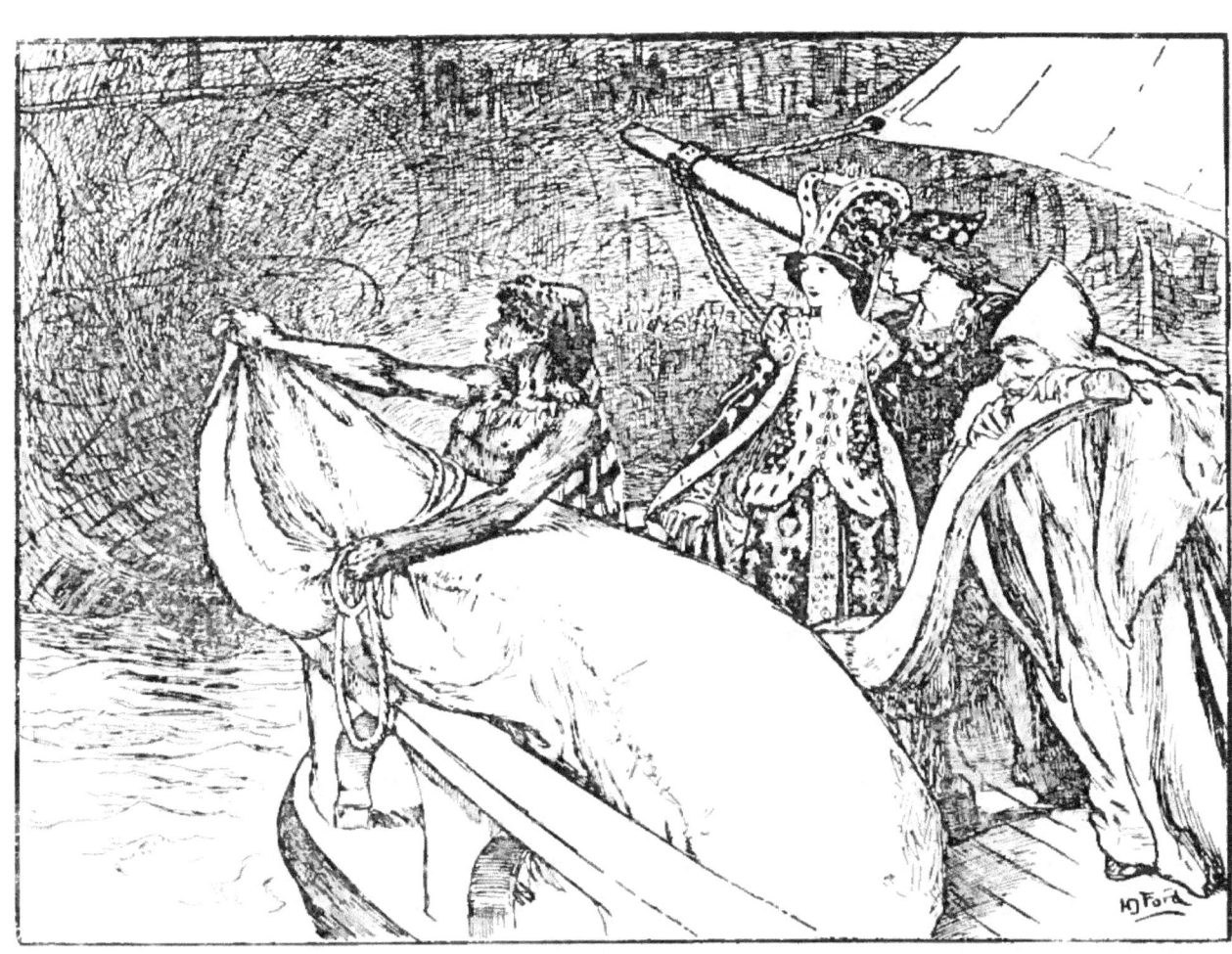

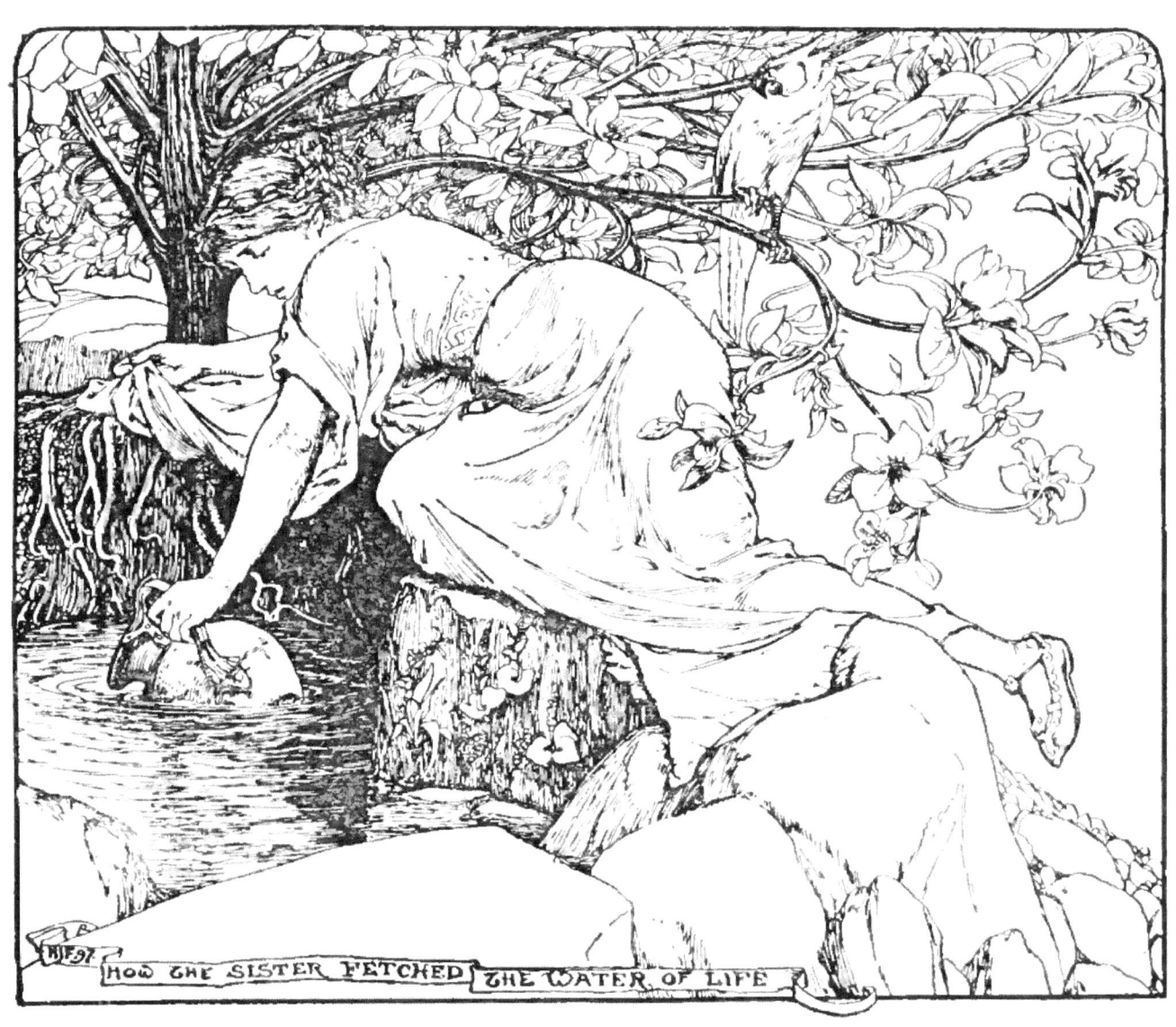

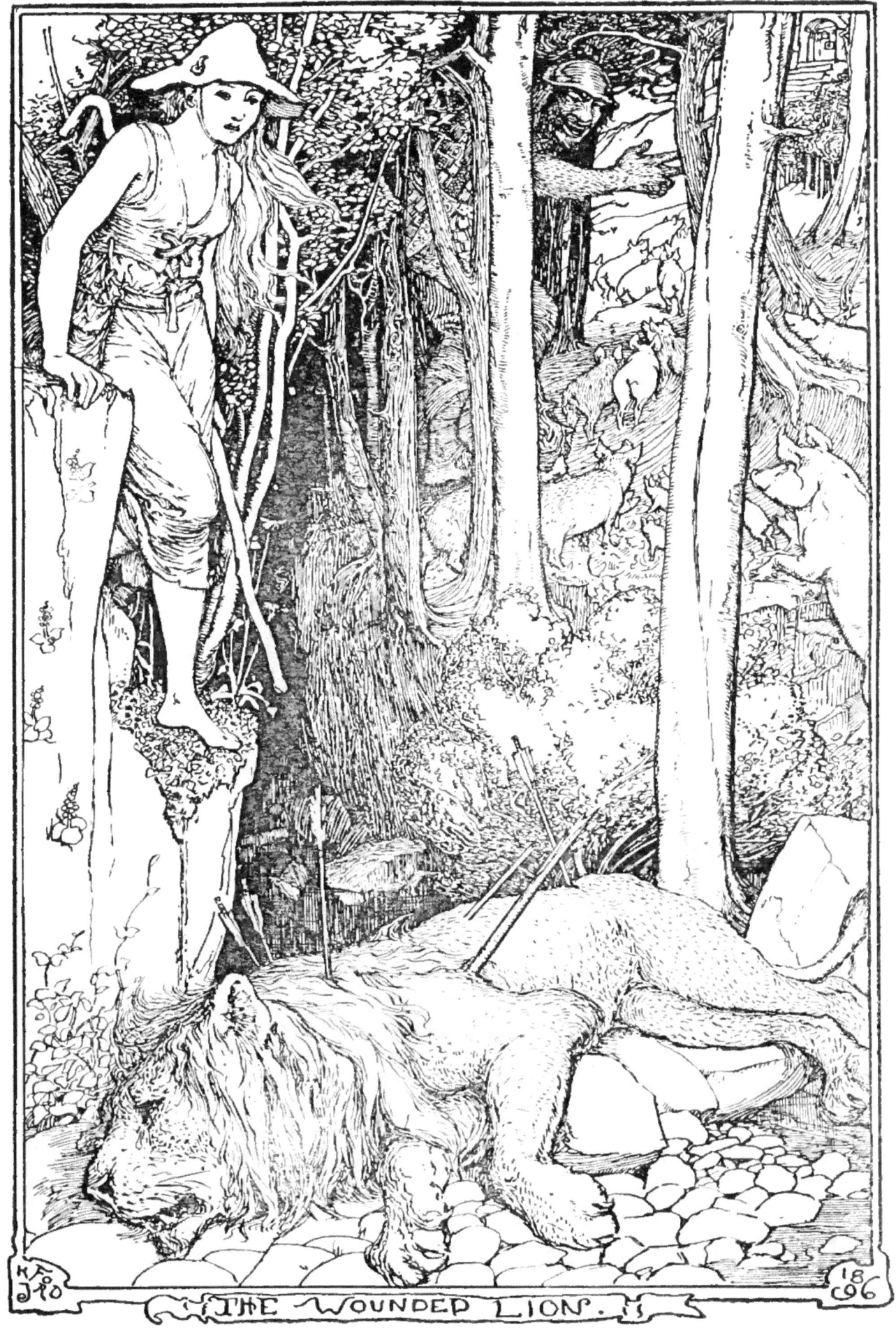
THE WOUNDED LION.

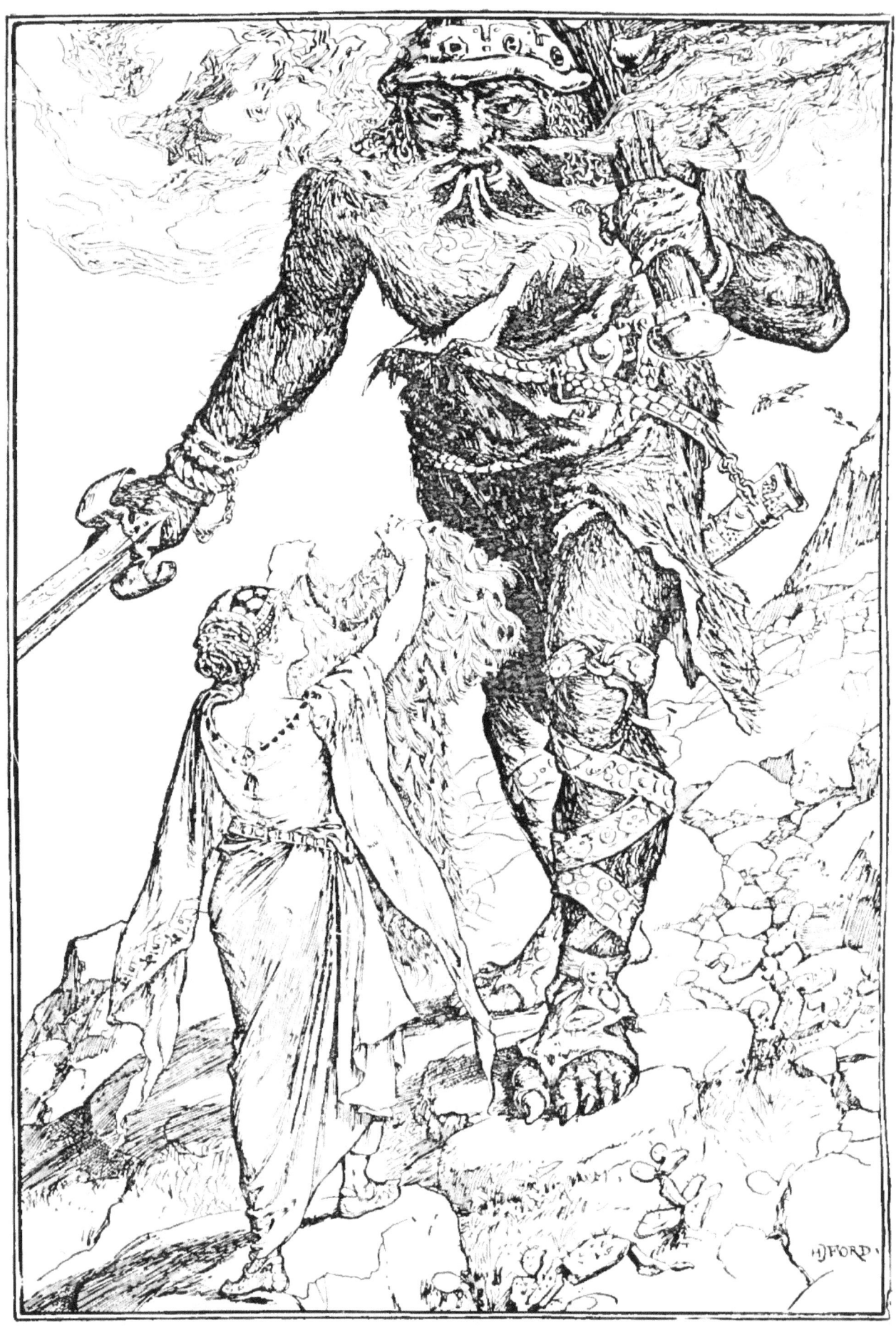

THE MAIDEN BRINGS THE COAT OF HAIR TO THE GIANT.

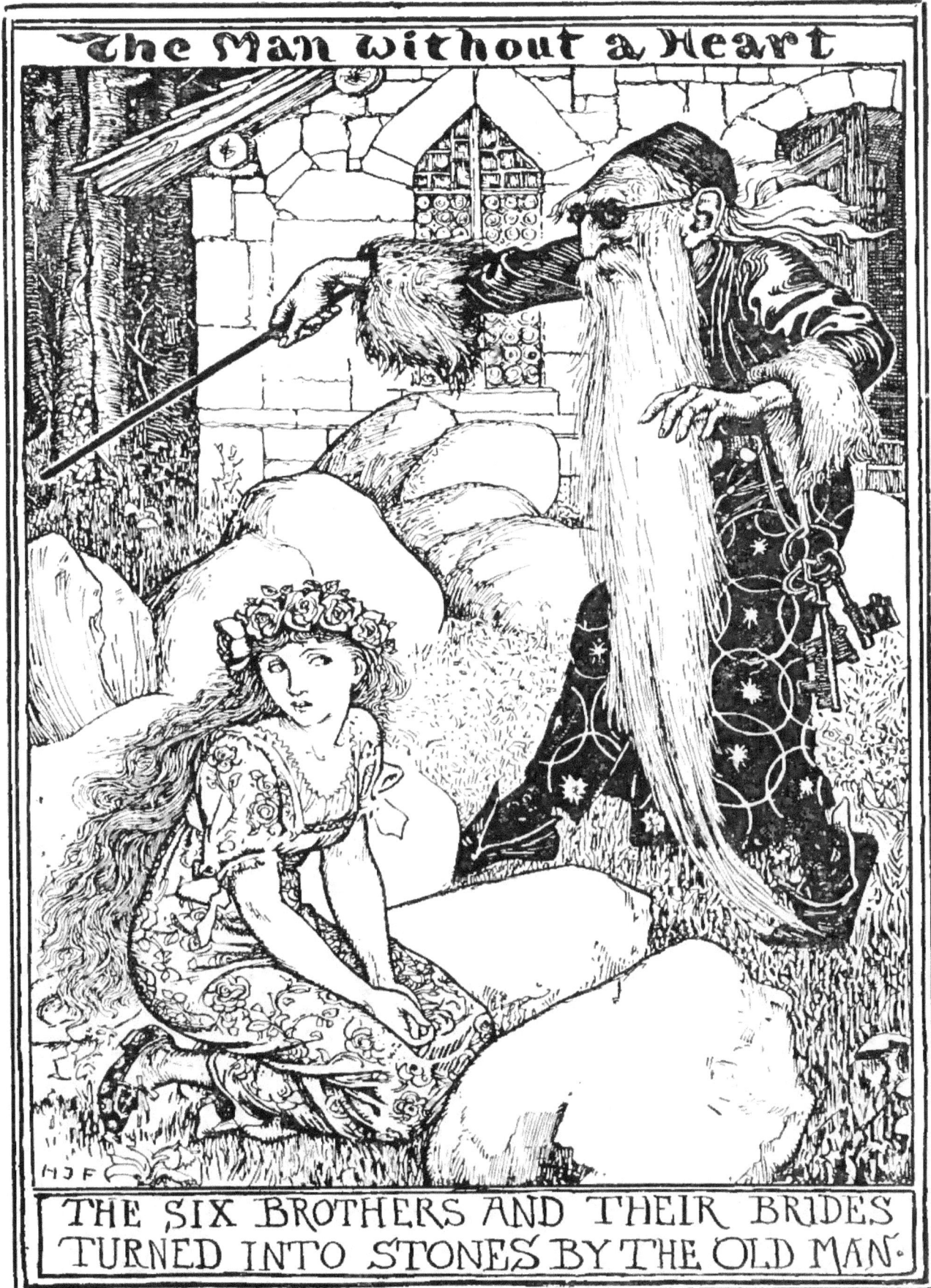

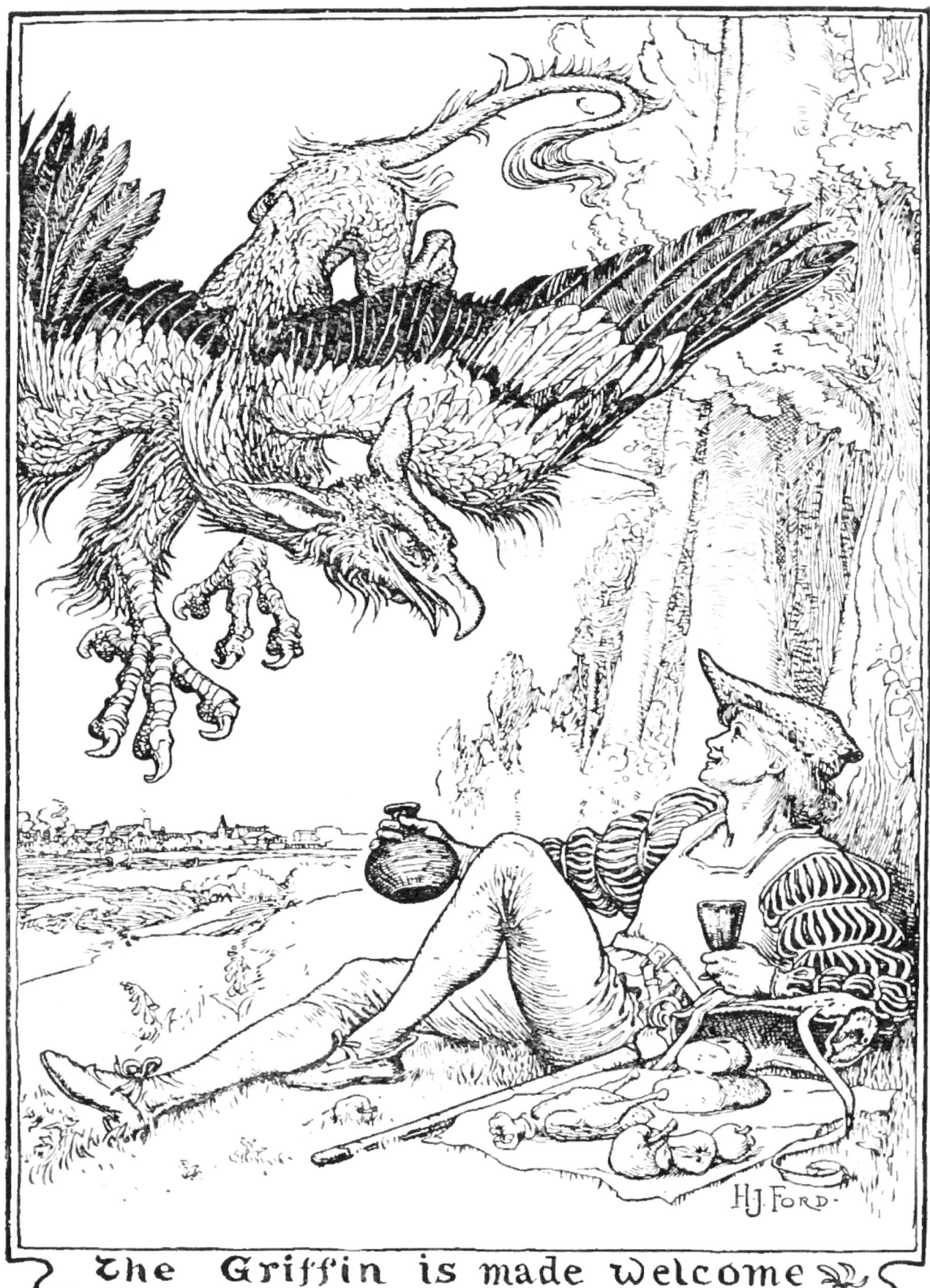

The Griffin is made welcome

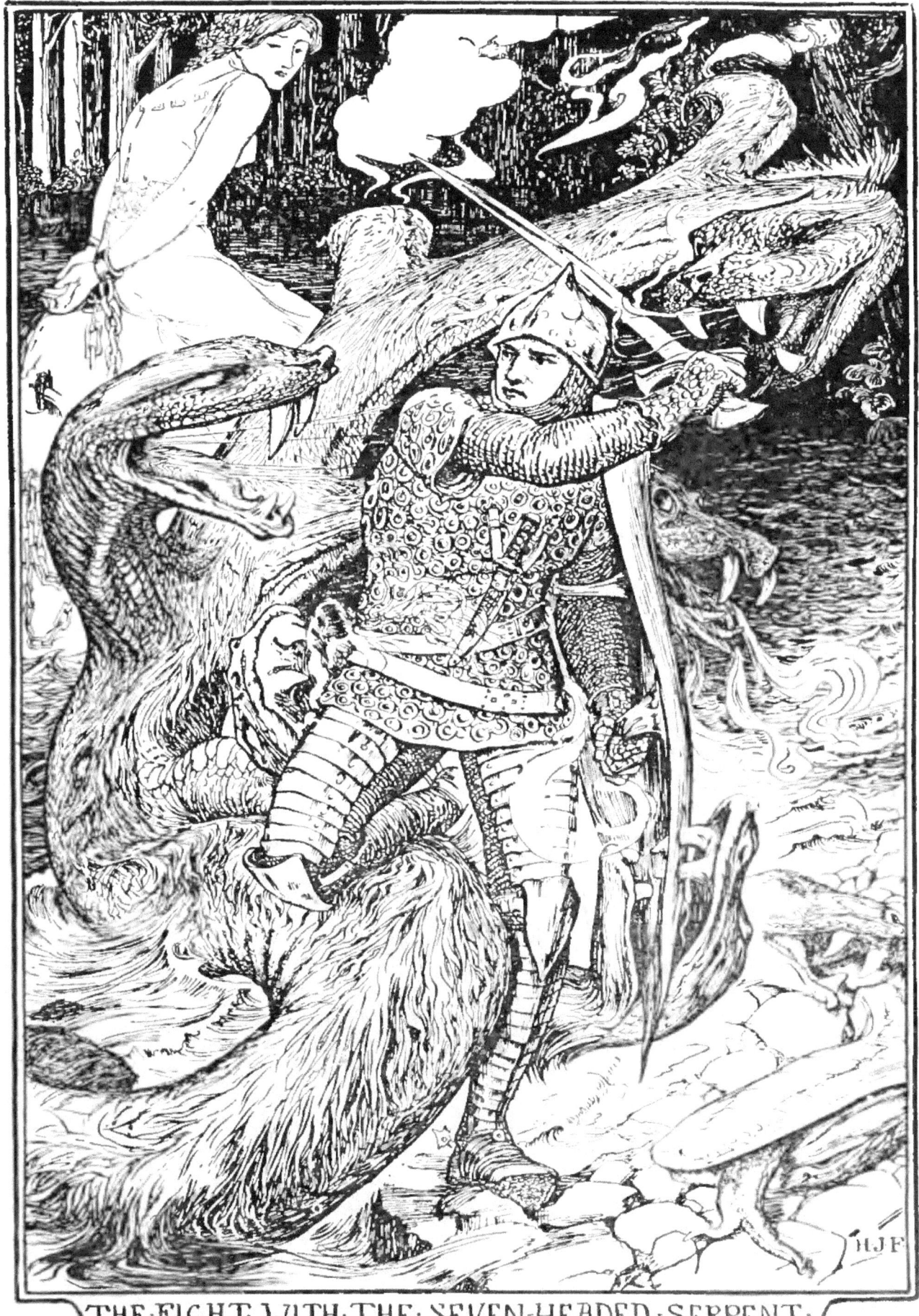

THE FIGHT WITH THE SEVEN-HEADED SERPENT

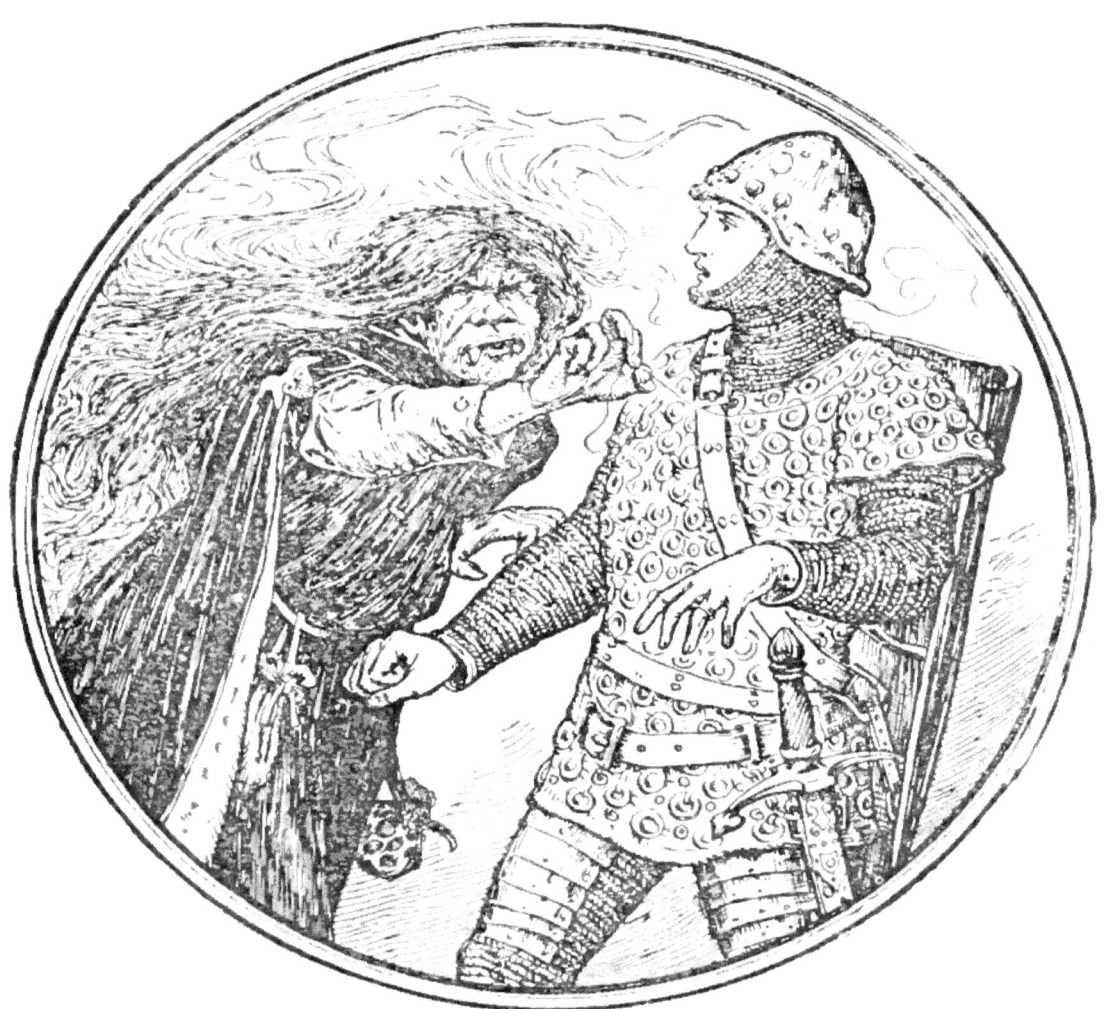

The Witch casts a spell on the Elder Brother.

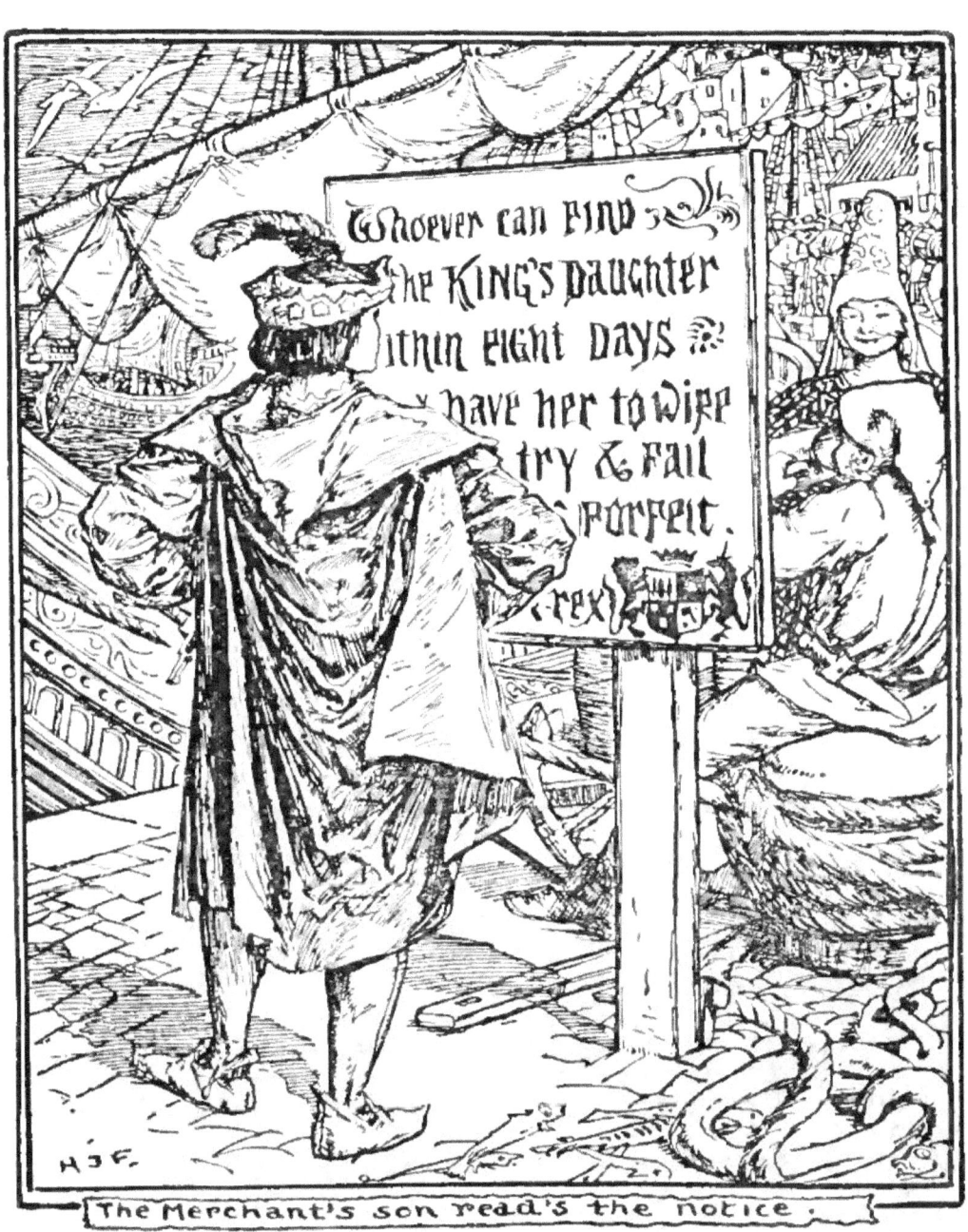

The Merchant's son reads the notice.

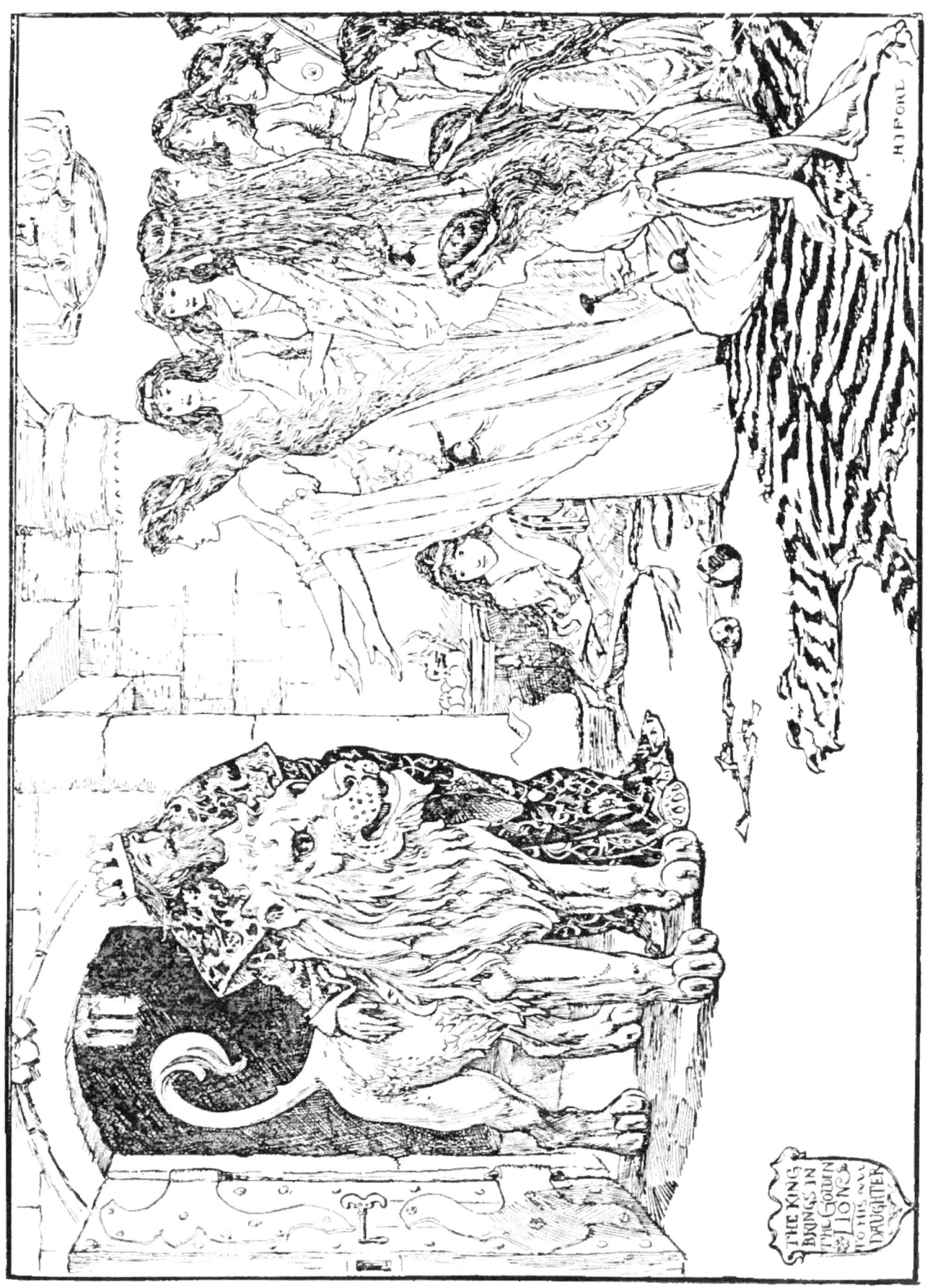
THE KING BRINGS IN THE GOLDEN LIONS TO HIS DAUGHTER

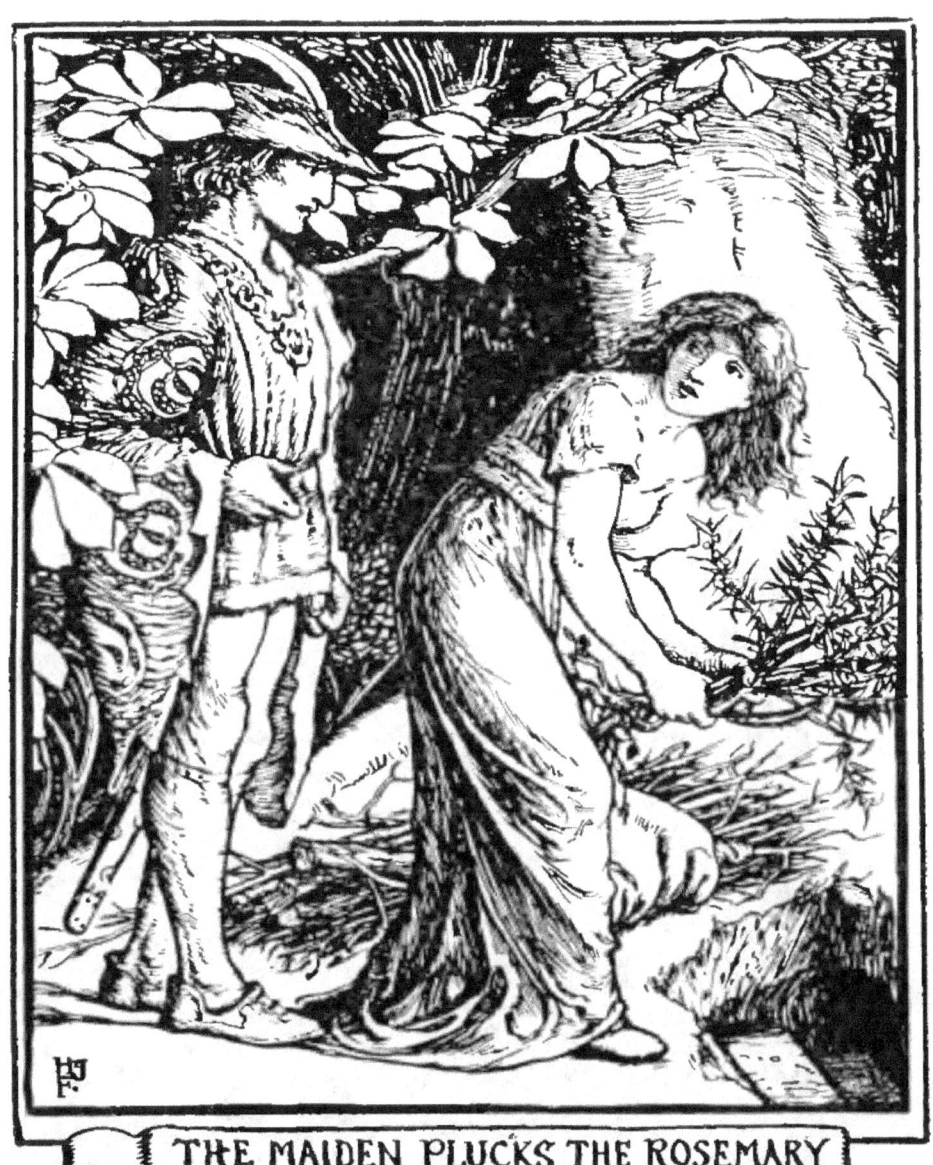
THE MAIDEN PLUCKS THE ROSEMARY

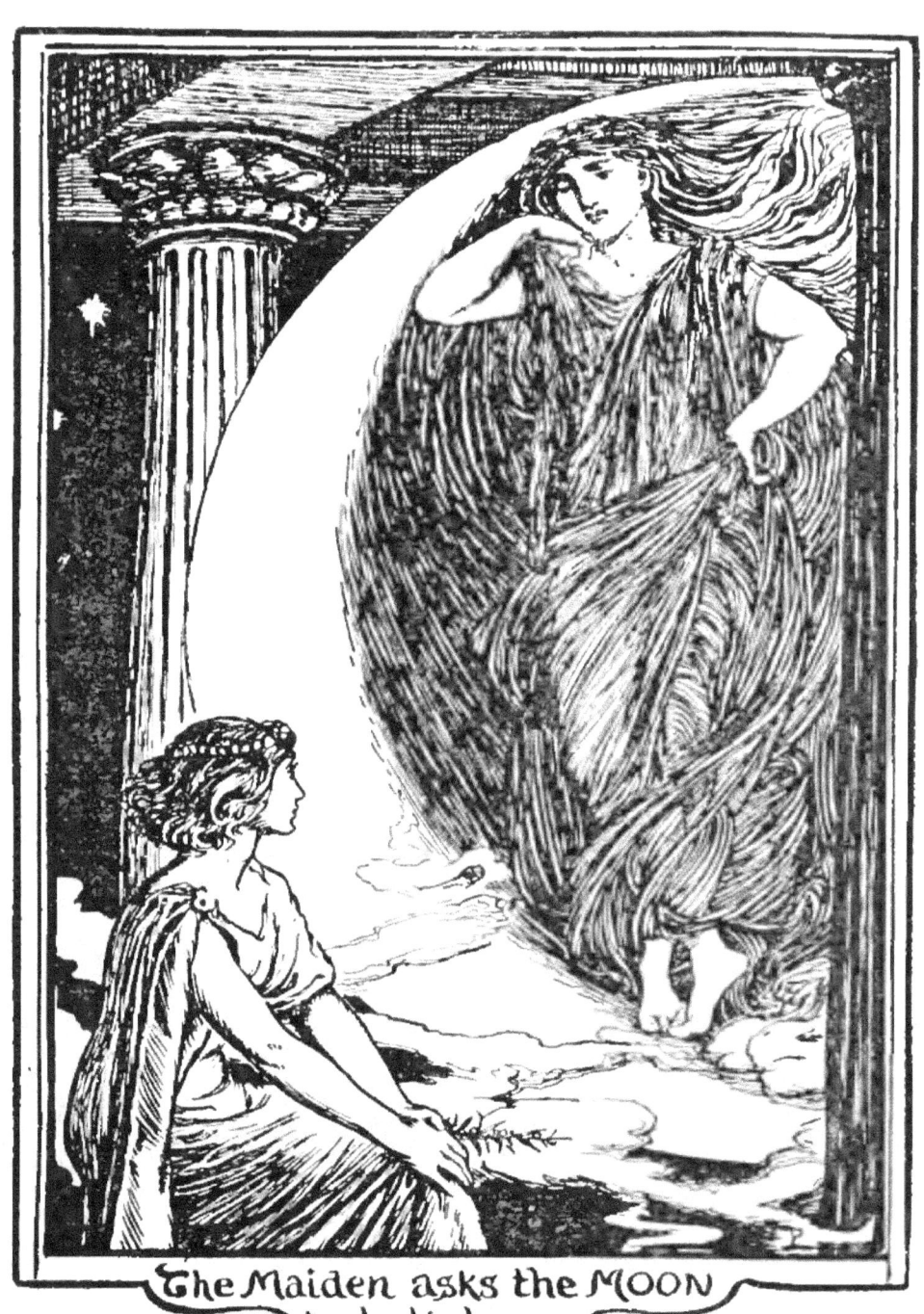
The Maiden asks the MOON to help her.

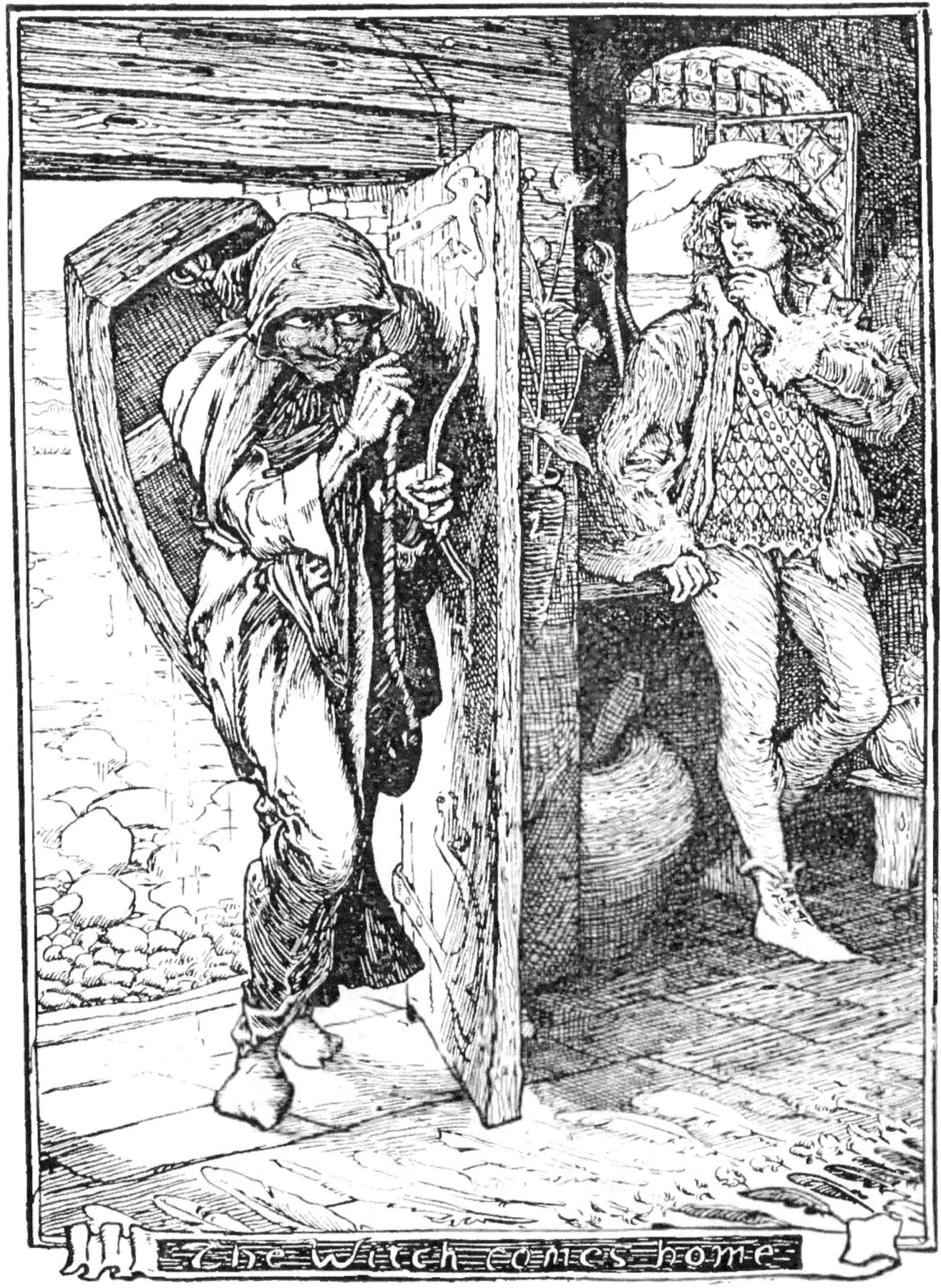

The Witch comes home

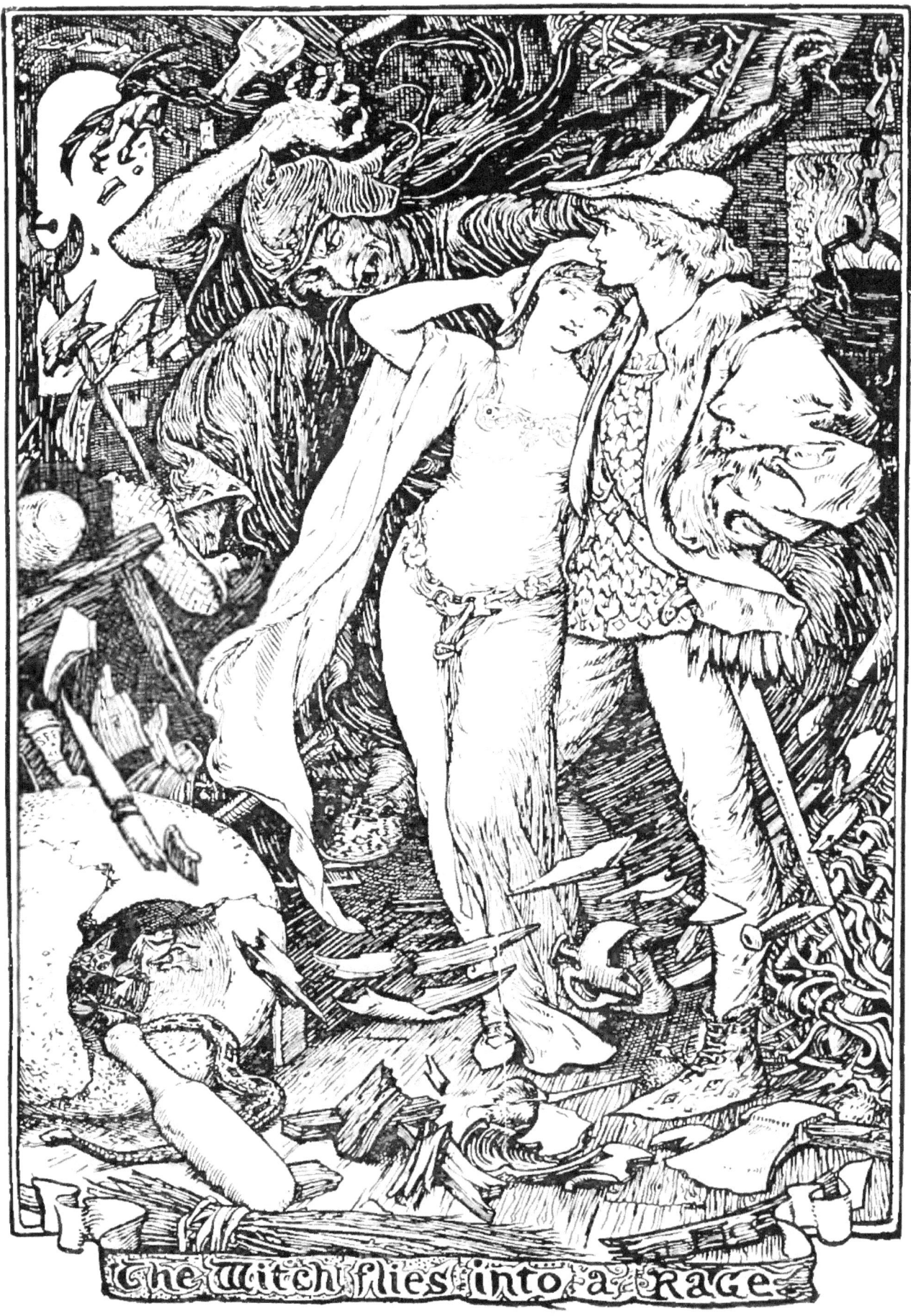

The Witch flies into a Rage

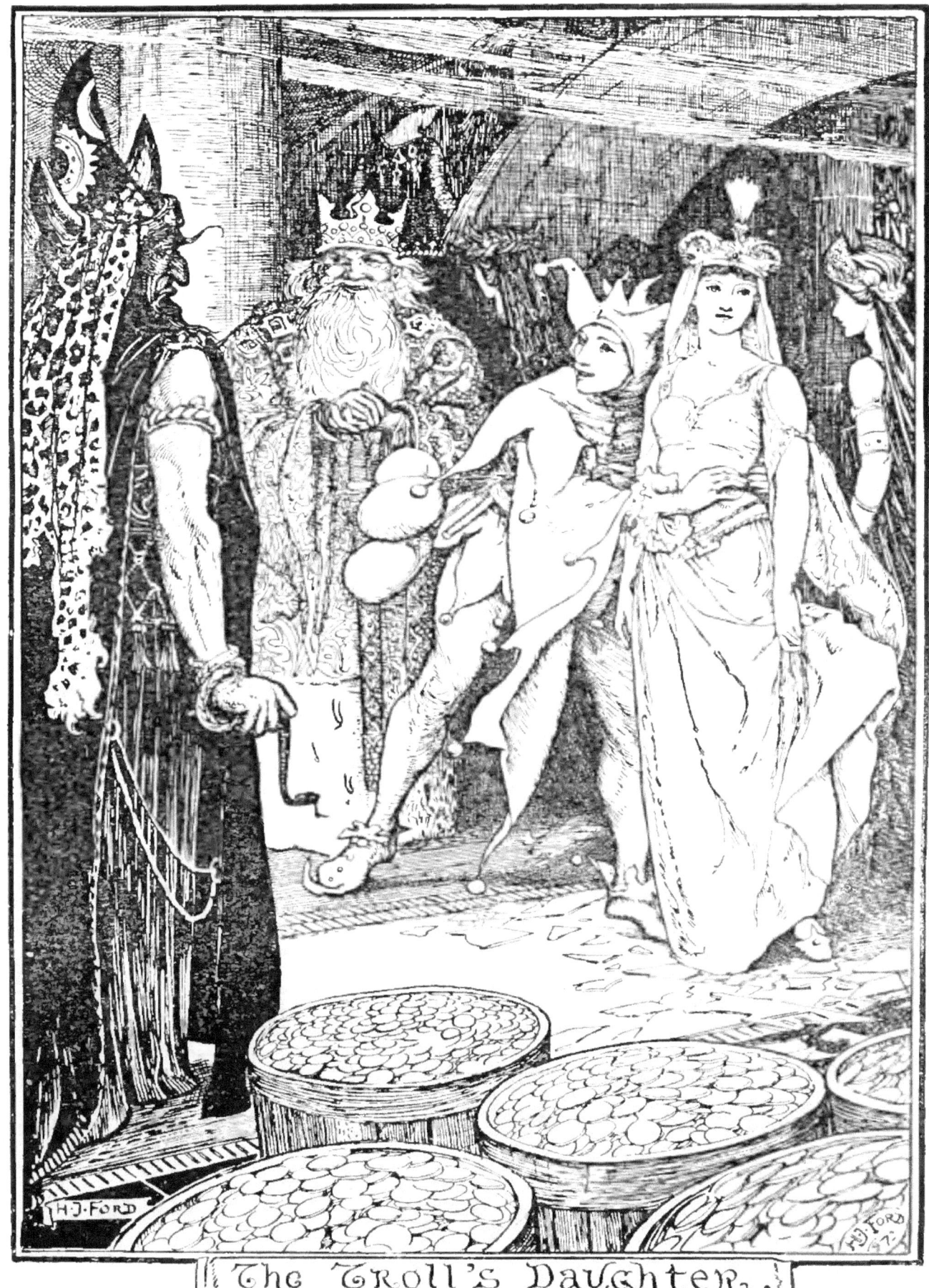

The Troll's Daughter.

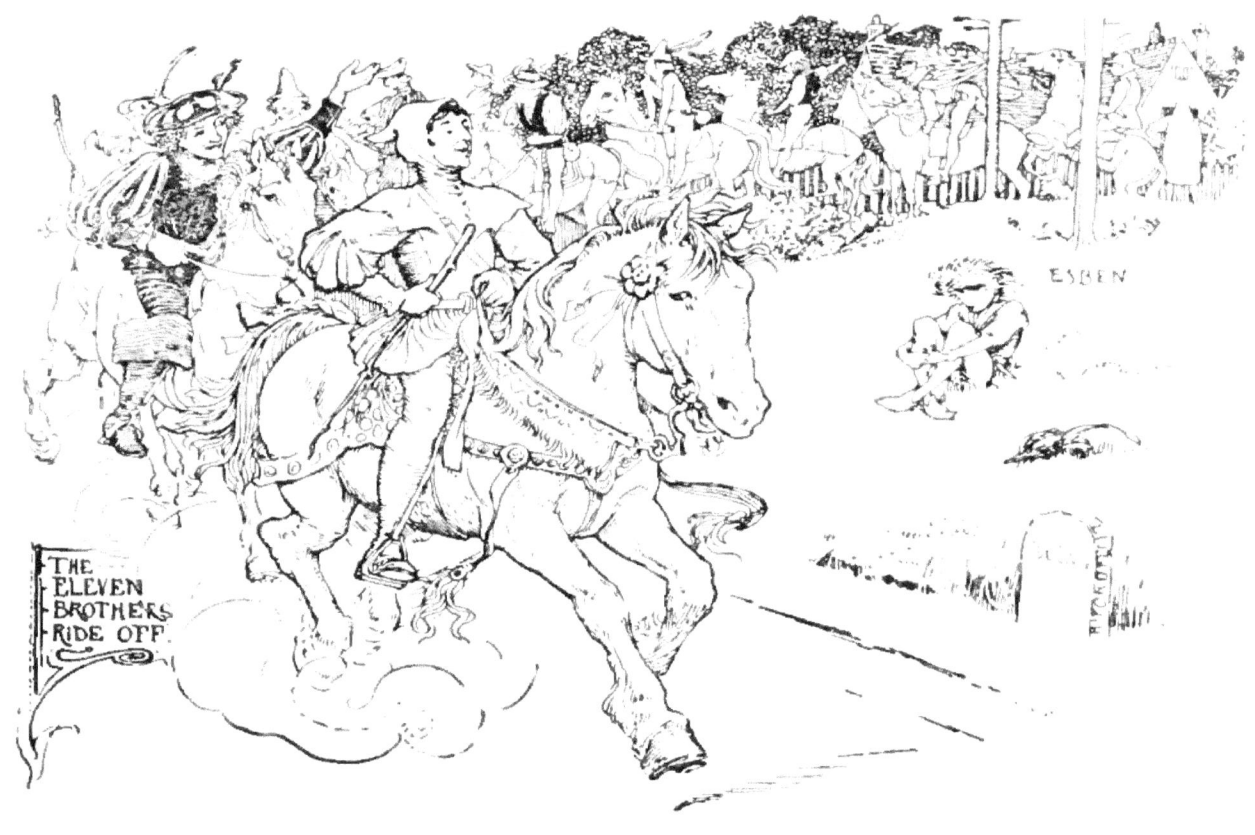

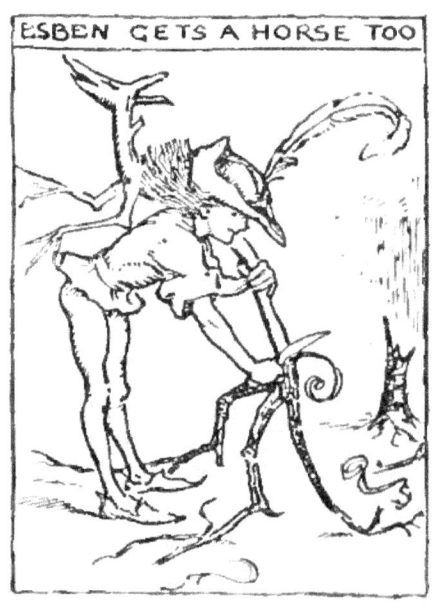

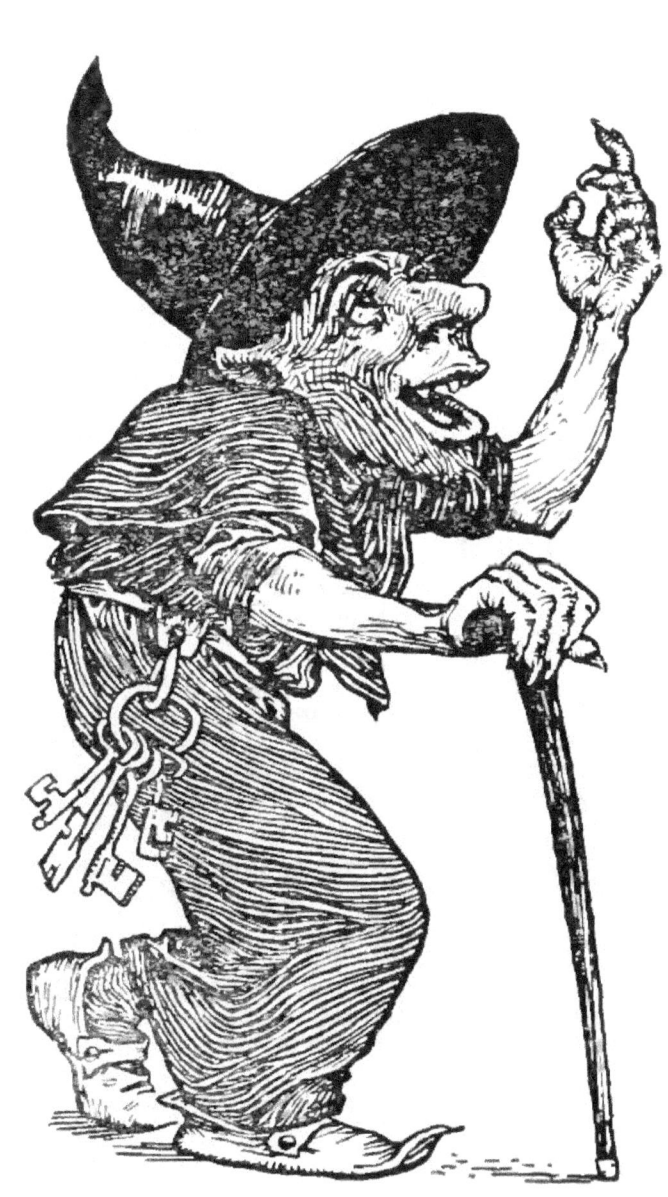

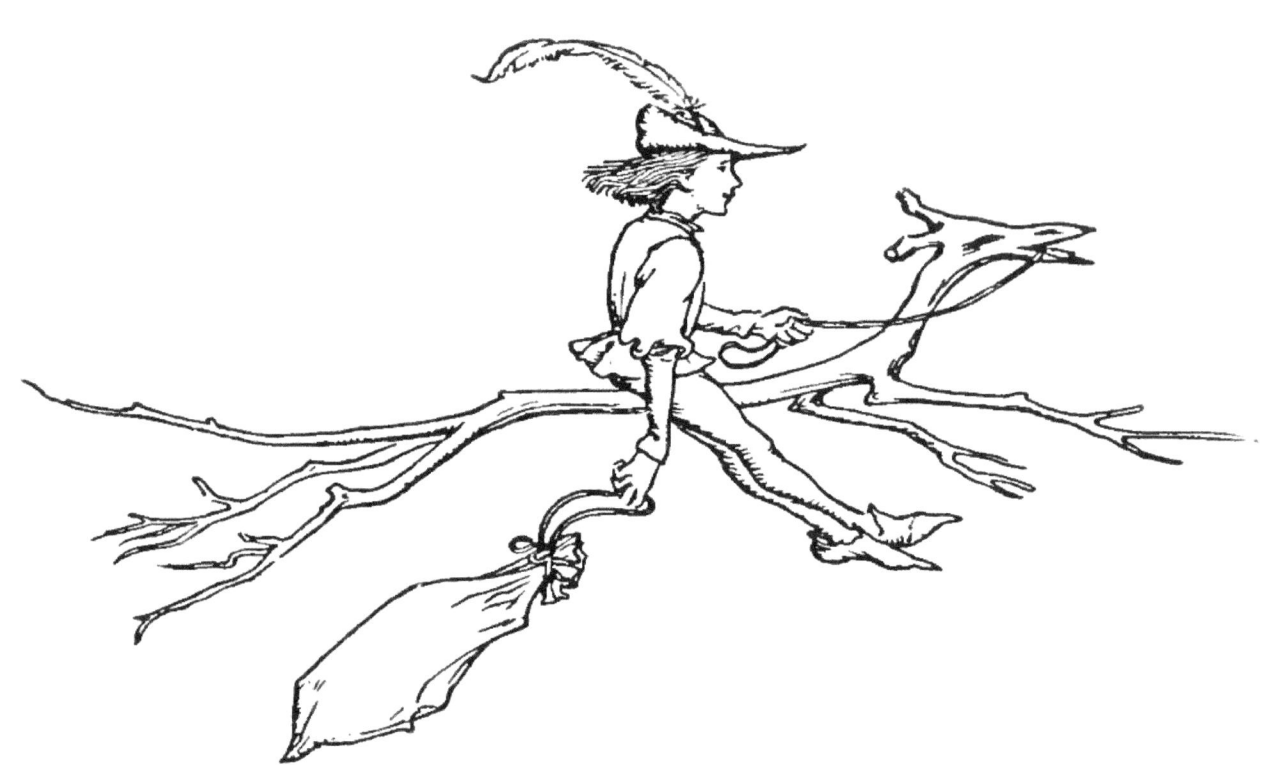

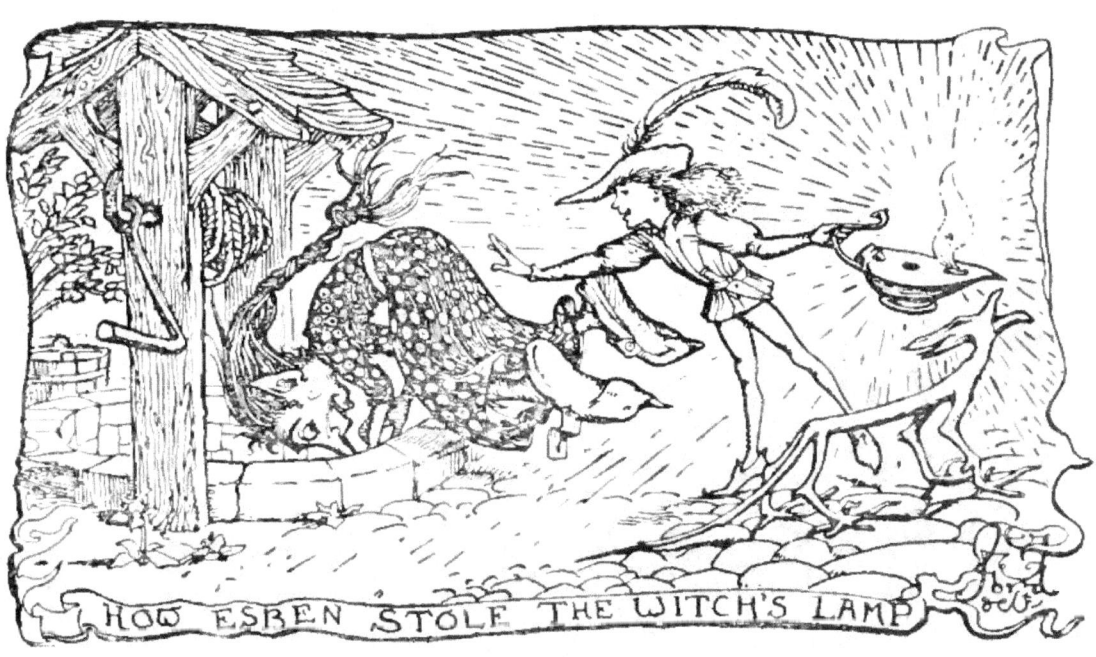
HOW ESBEN STOLE THE WITCH'S LAMP

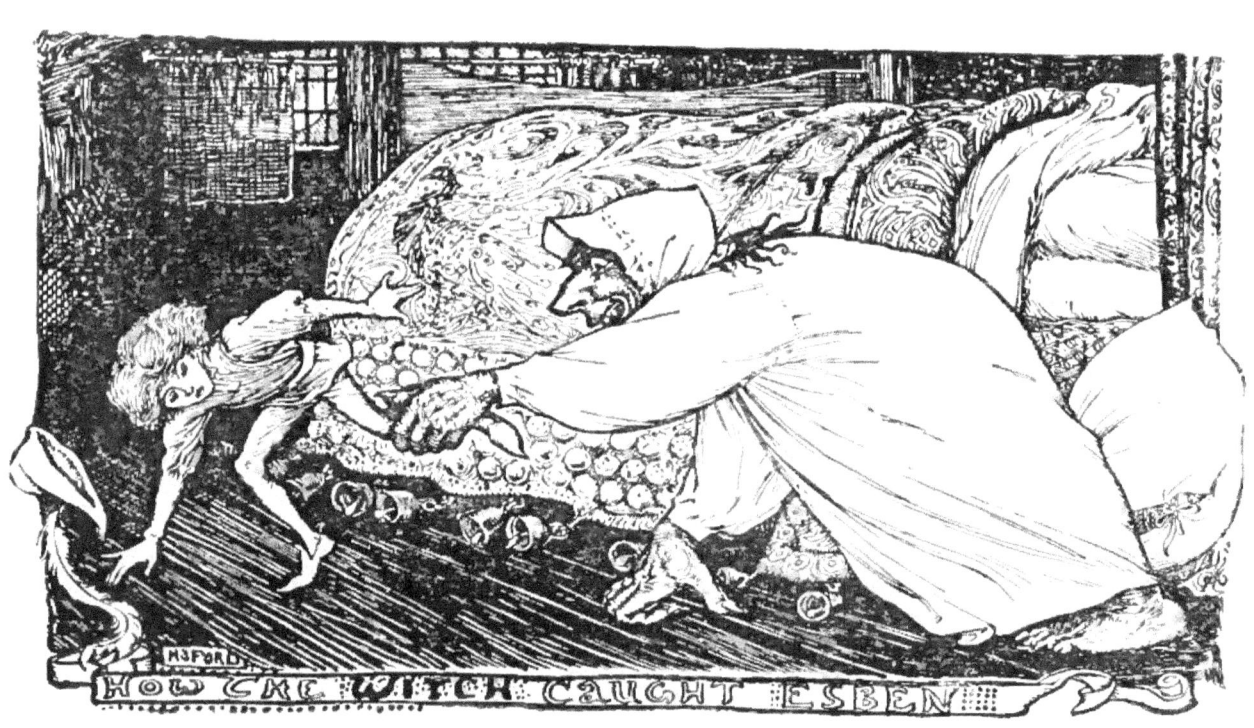
HOW THE WITCH CAUGHT ESBEN

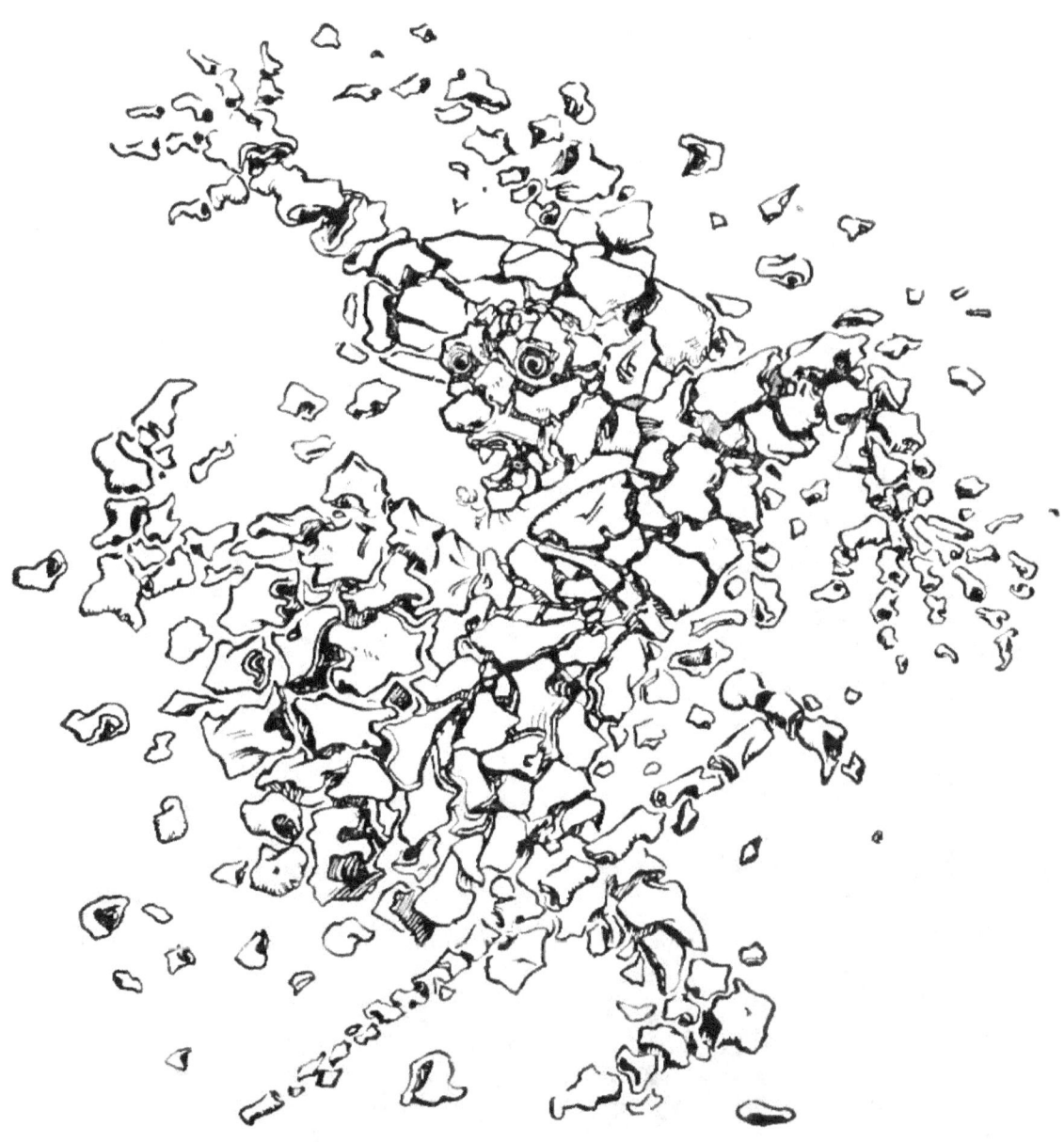

The Witch breaks into Flints

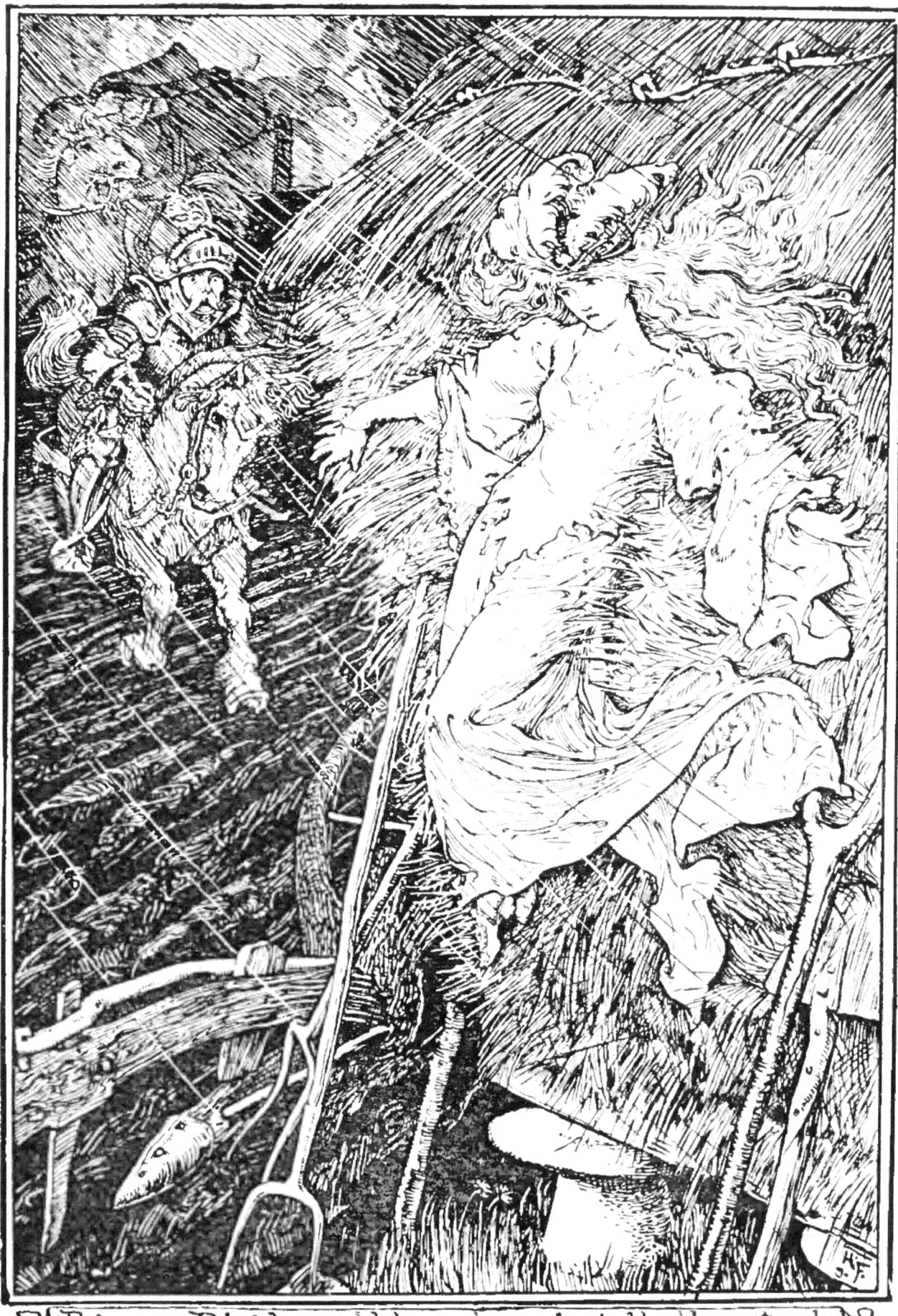

Princess Diaphana blown against the haystack

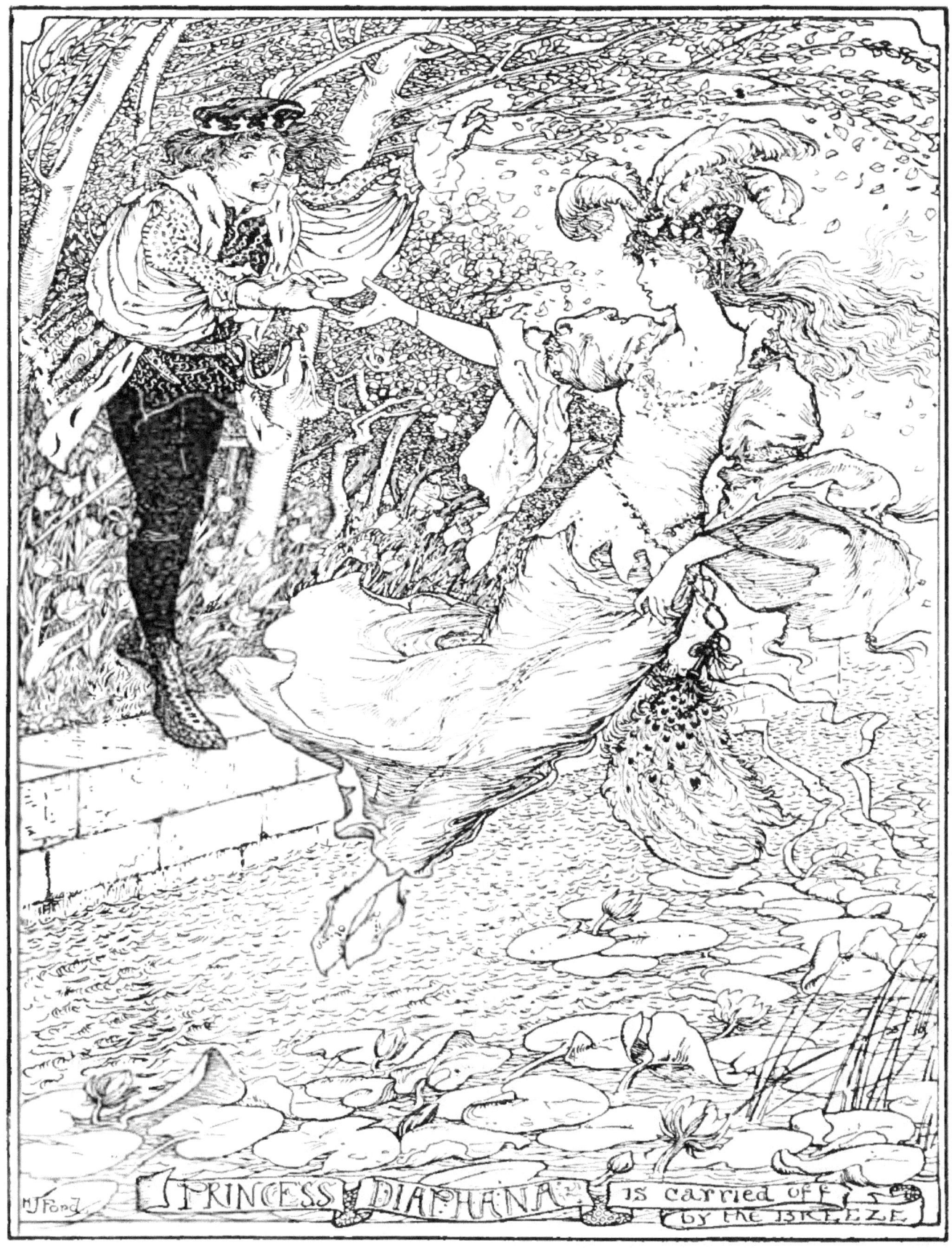

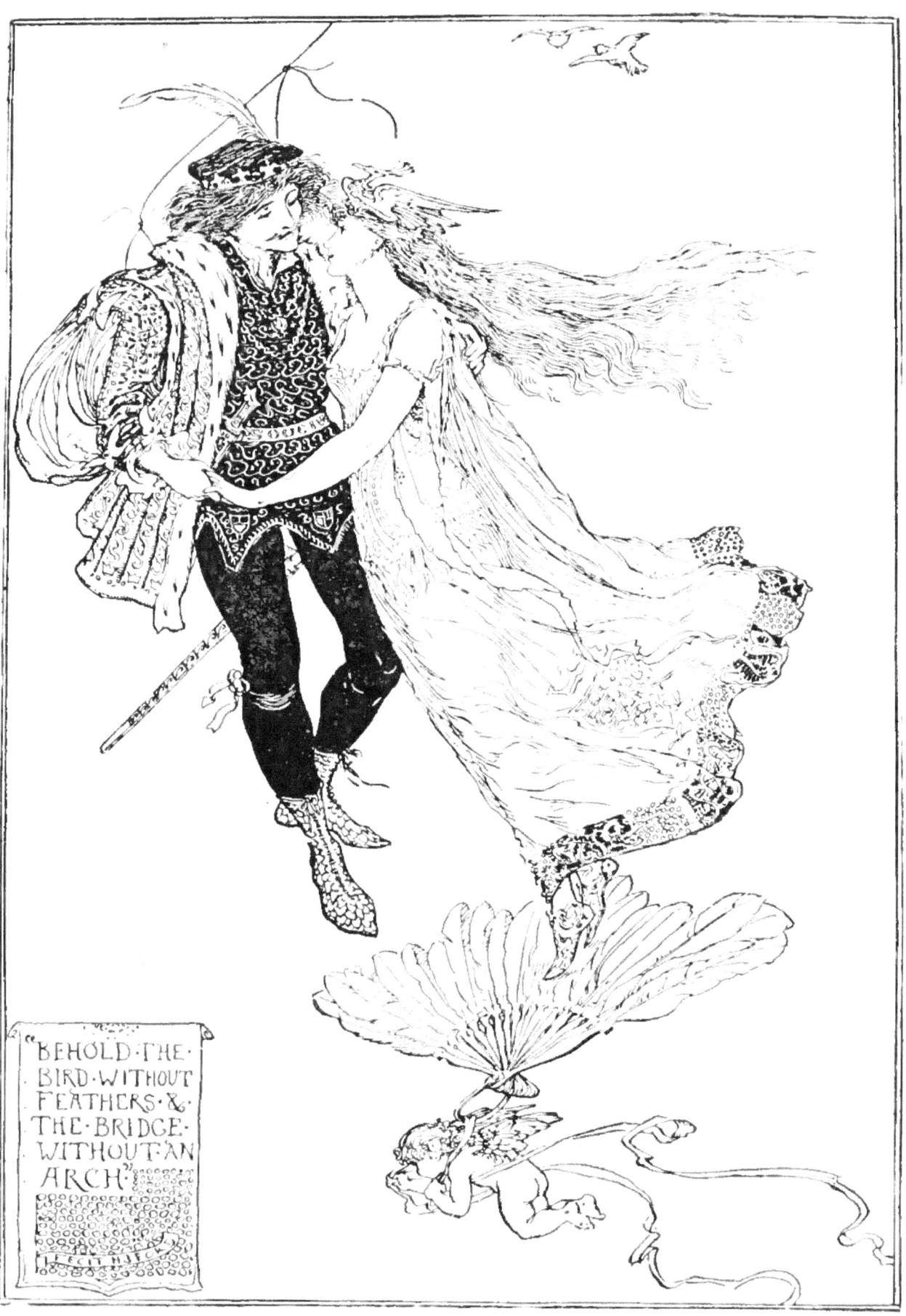

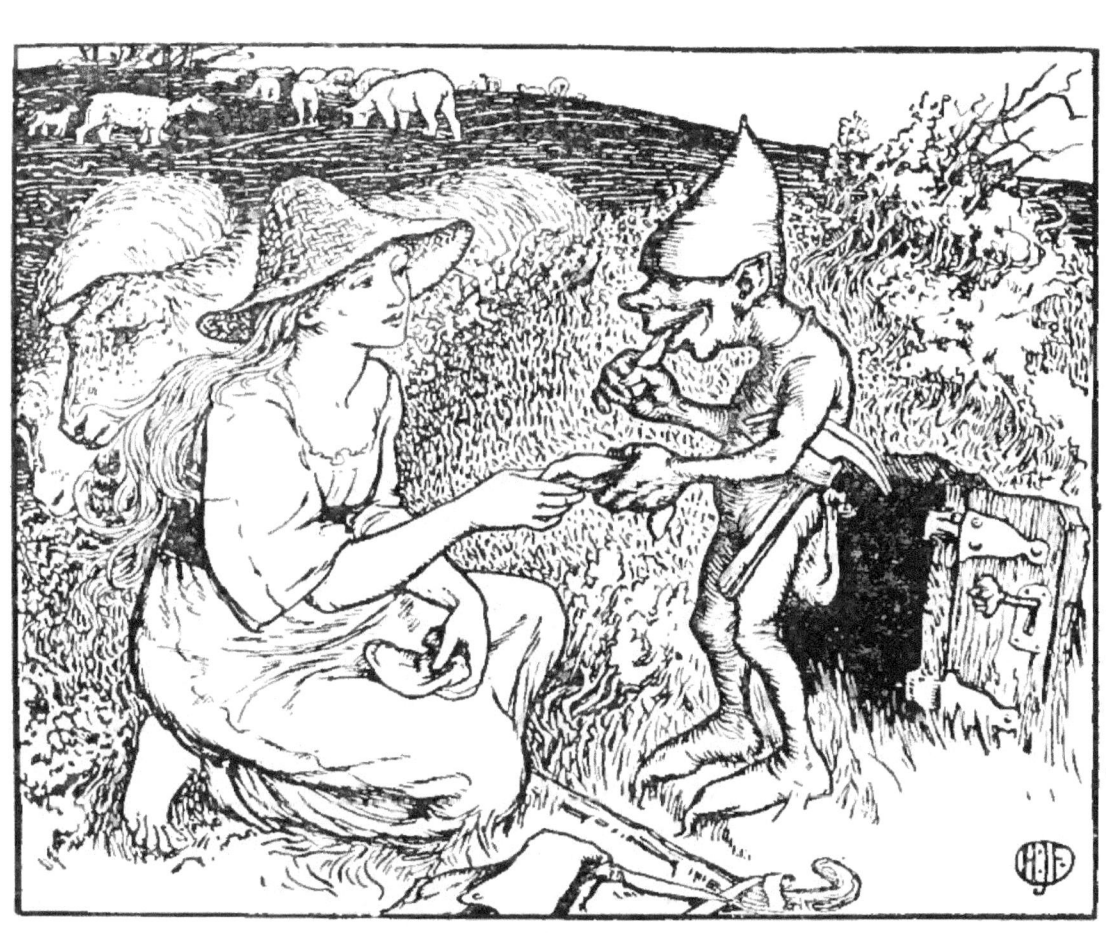

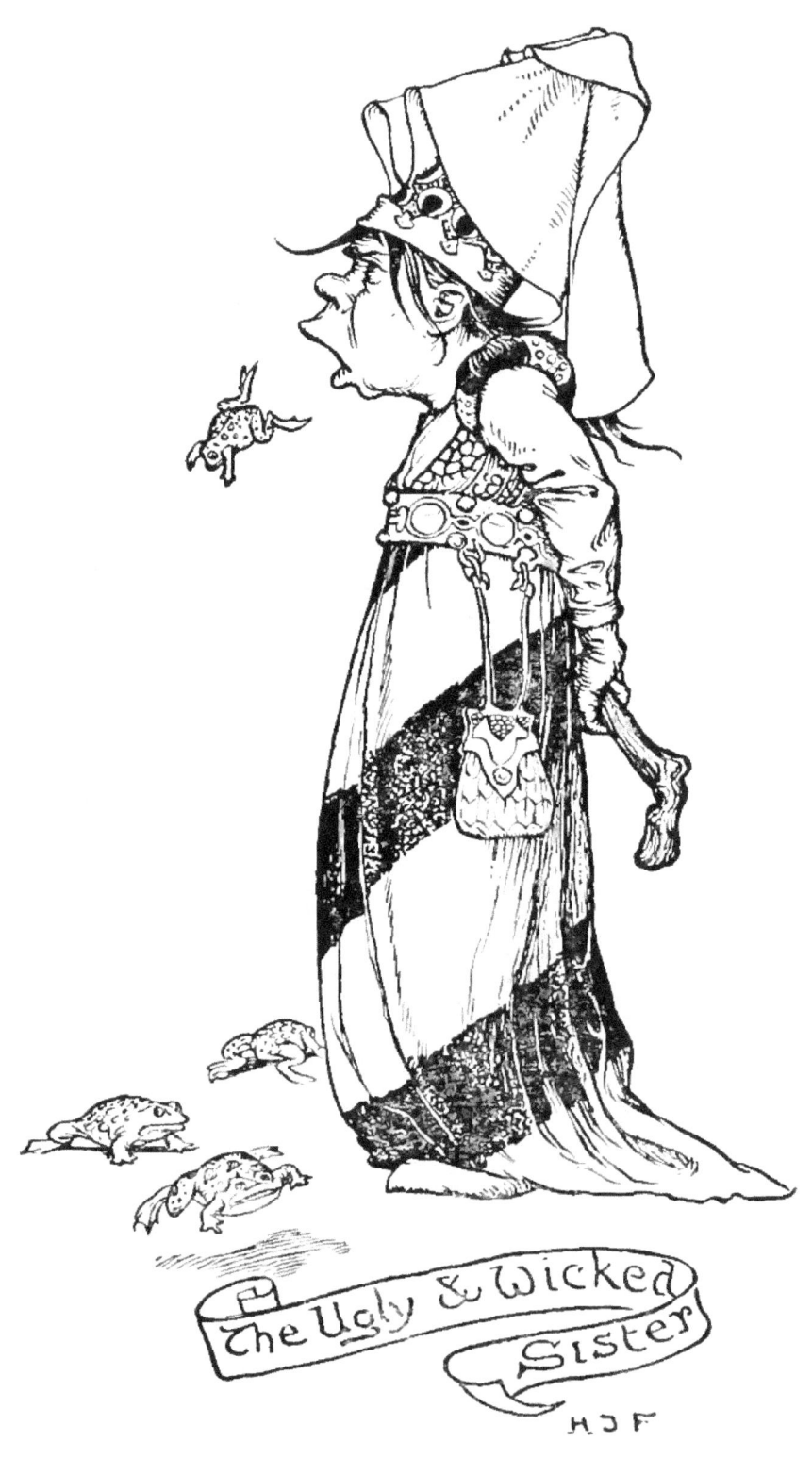

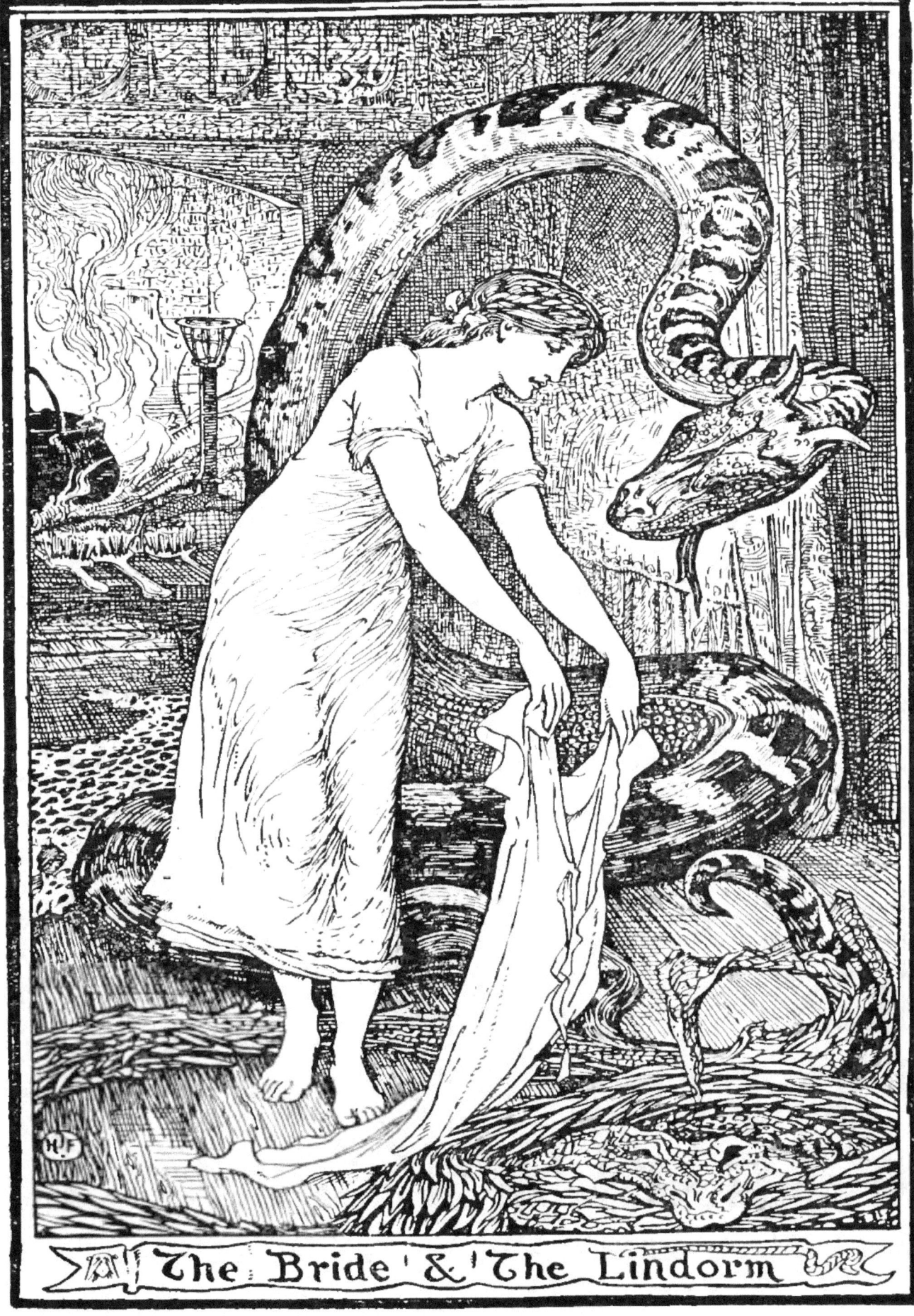

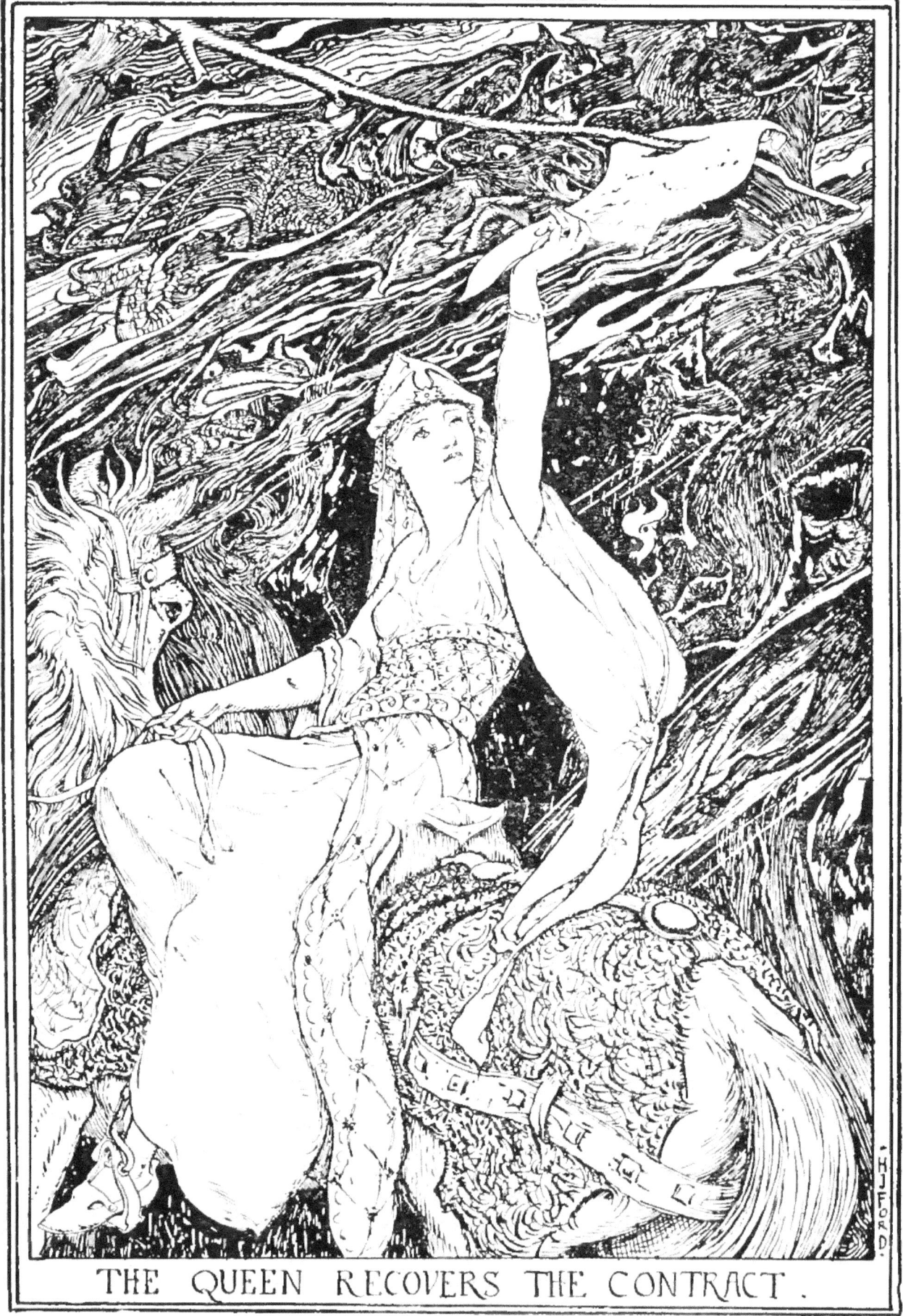

THE QUEEN RECOVERS THE CONTRACT.

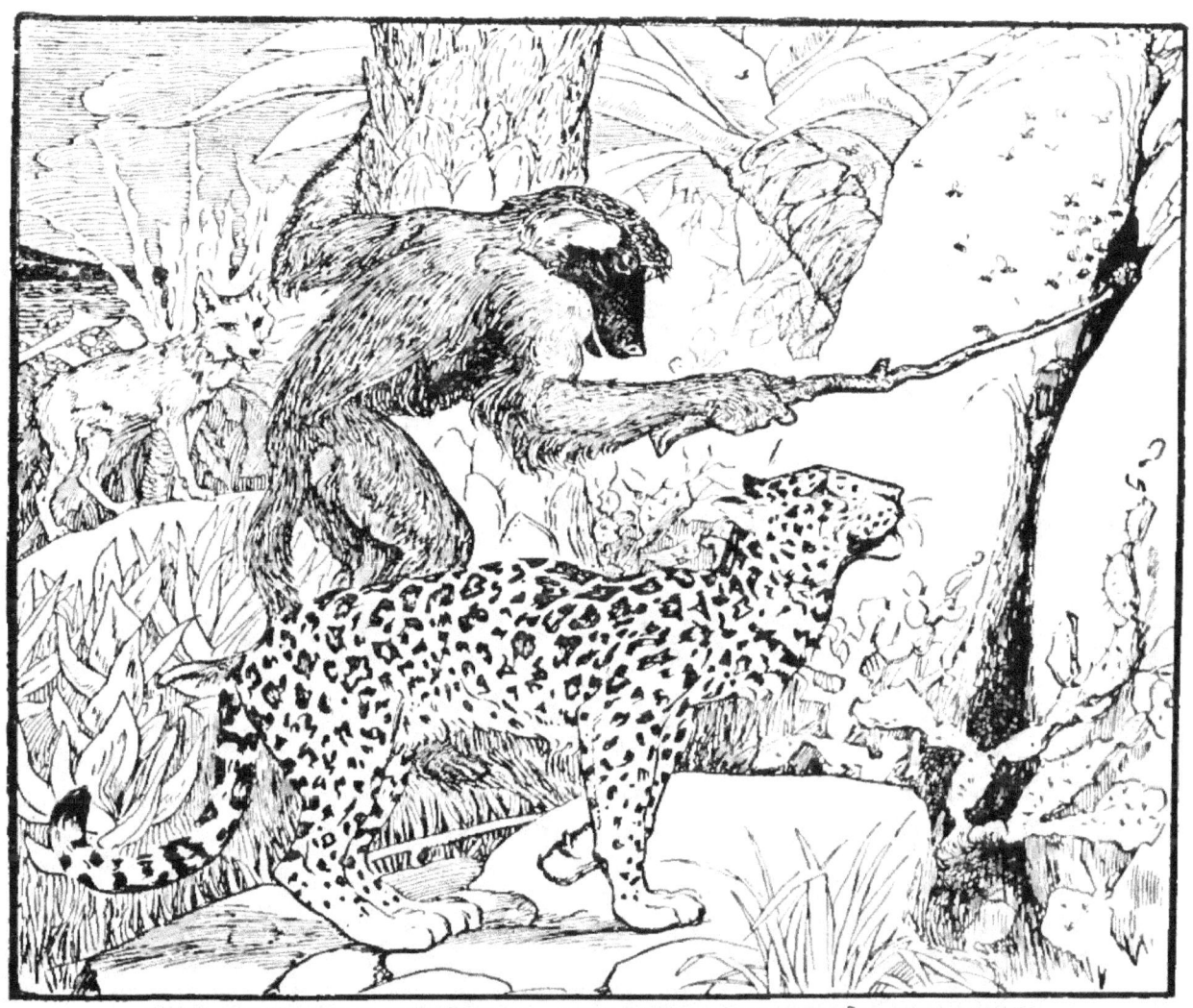

THE BABOON WISHES TO SEE THE PANTHER'S CHILDREN

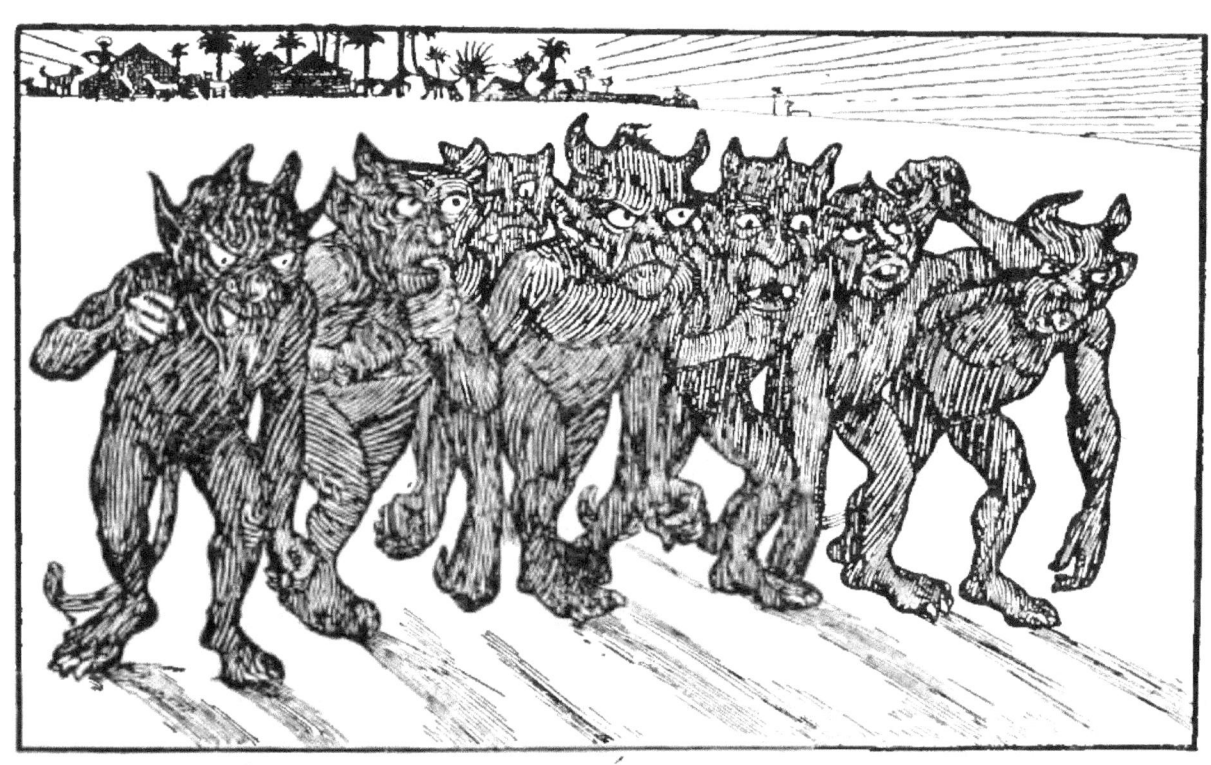

THE NYAMATSANÉS RETURN HOME

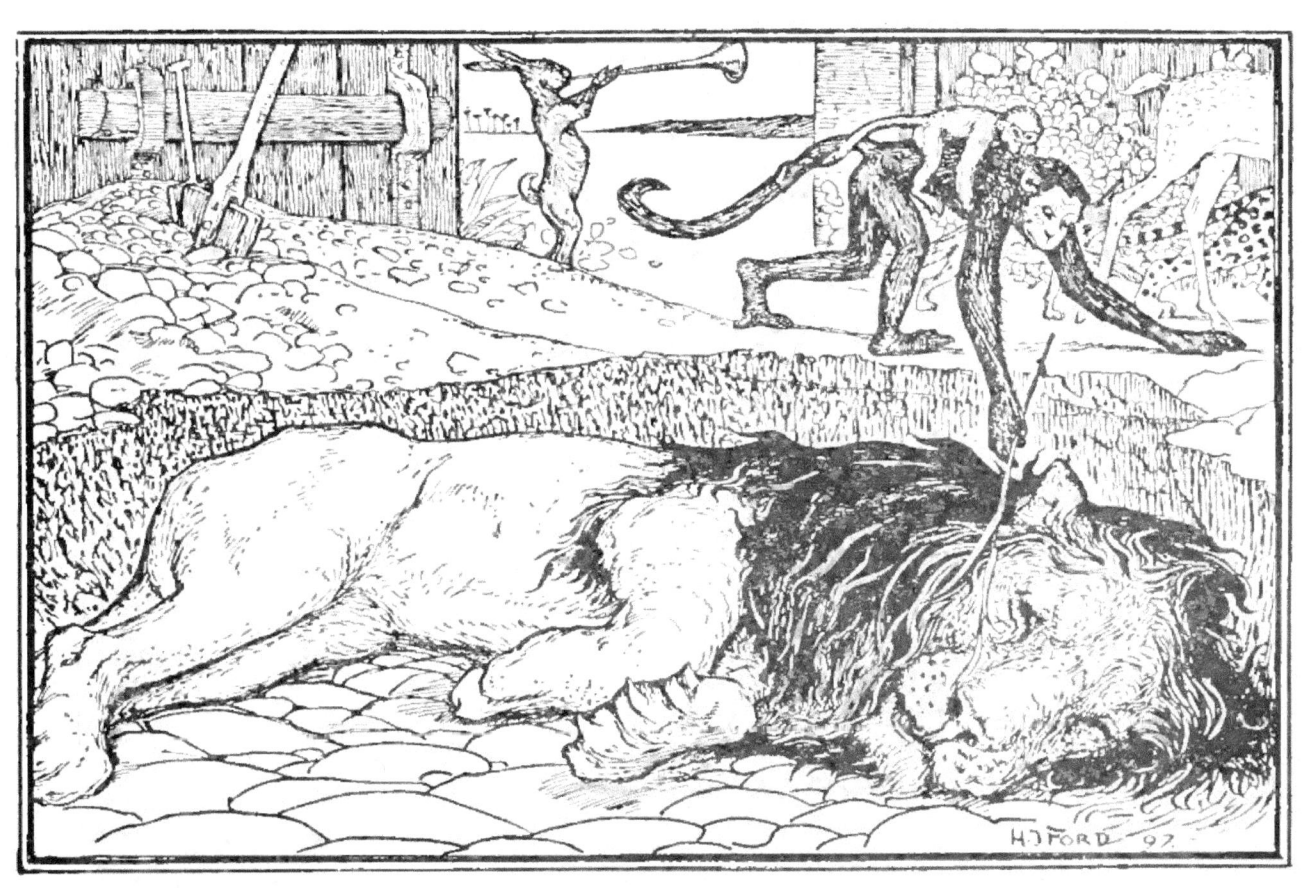

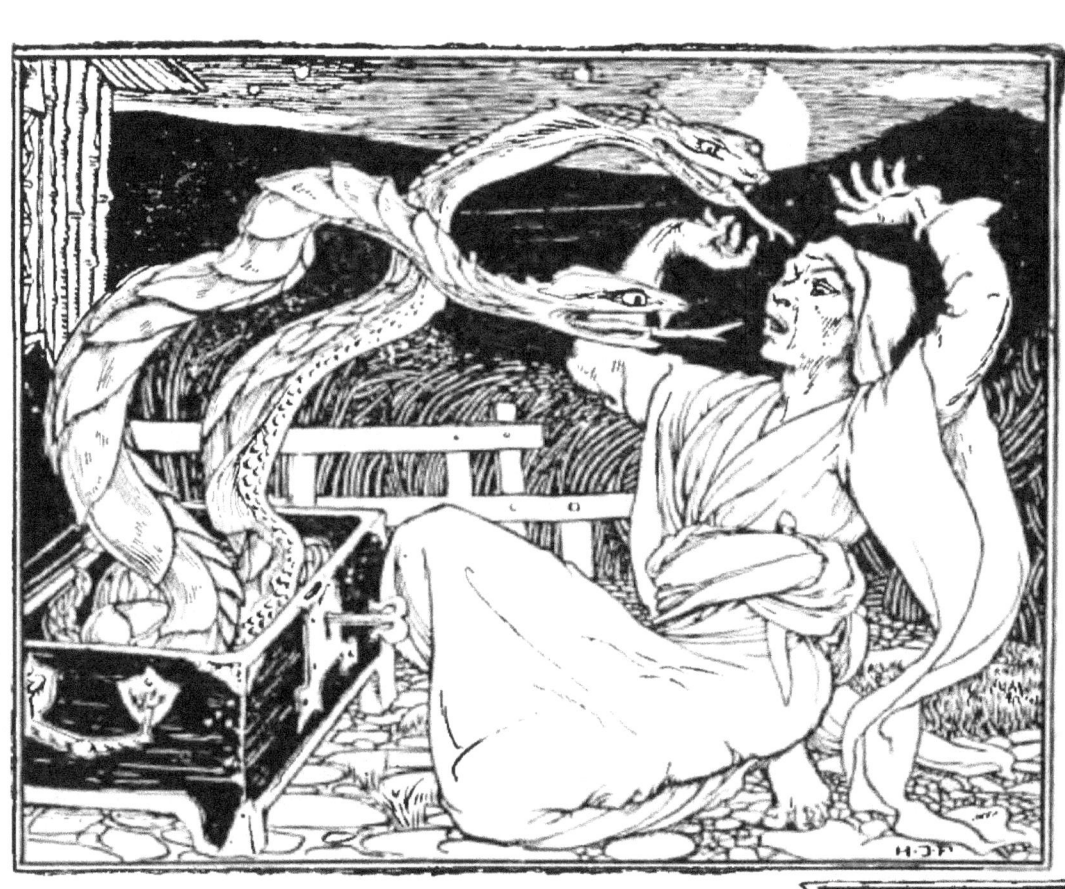

The Old Woman Opens the Box

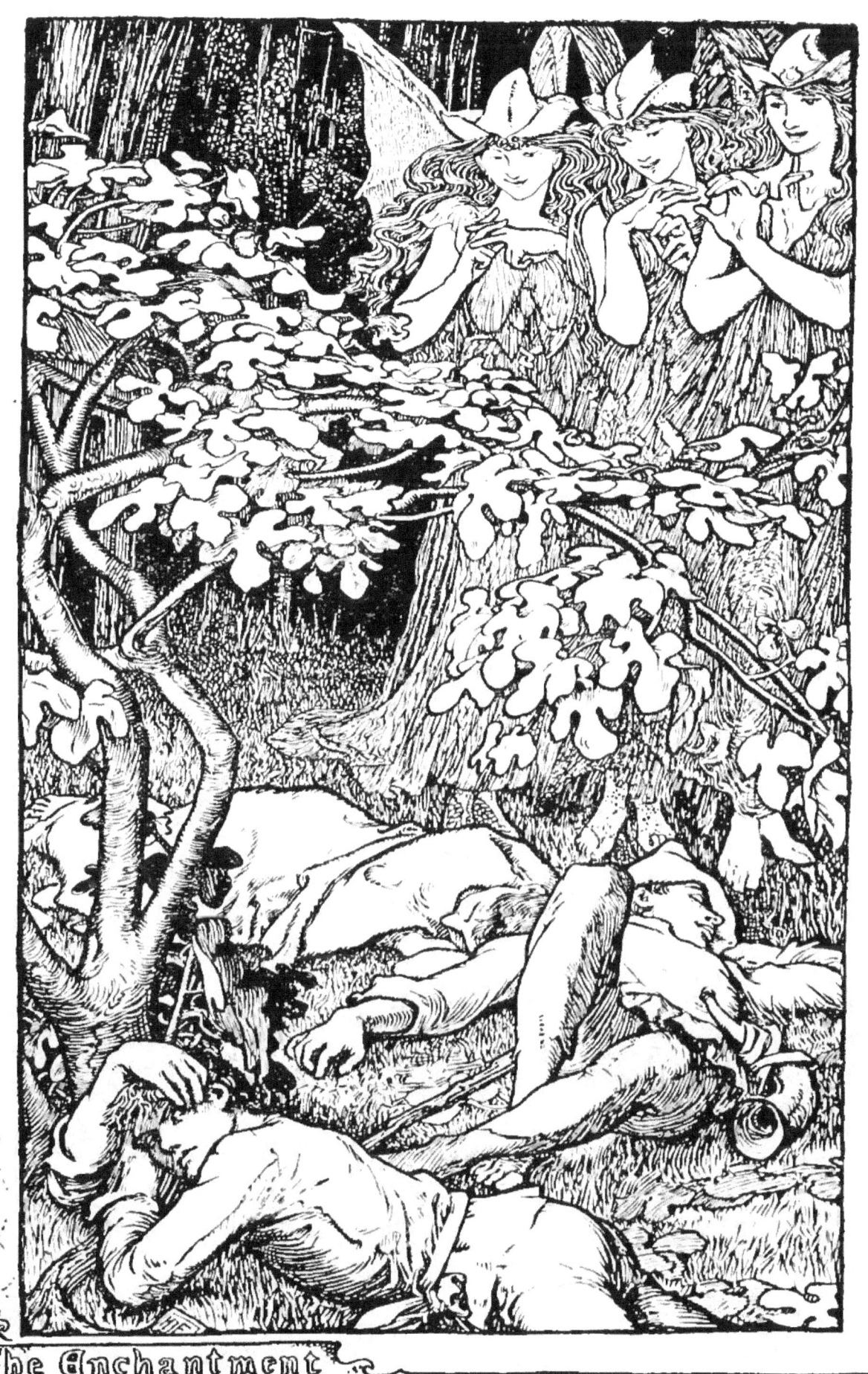
The Enchantment

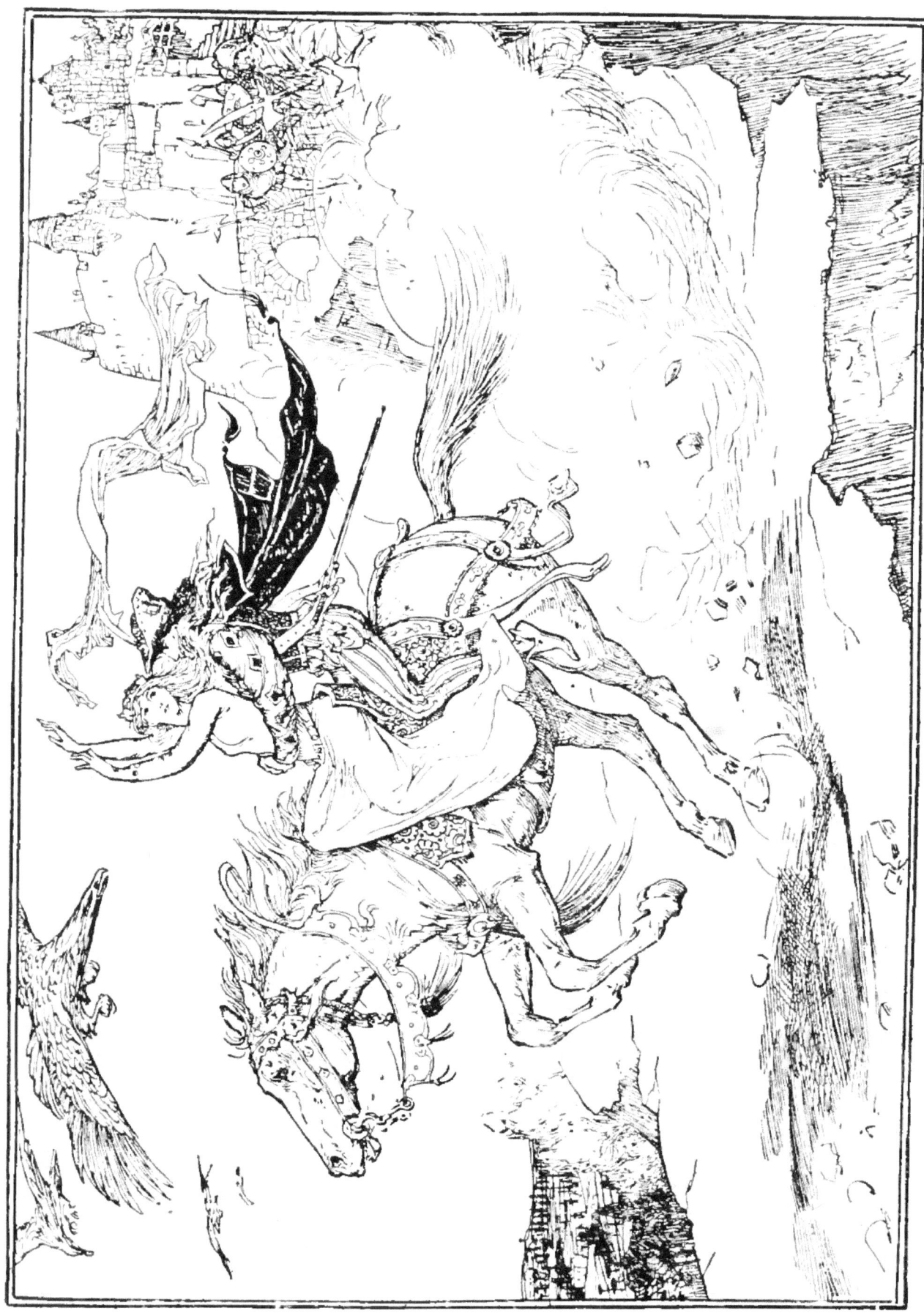

CICCU CARRIES OFF THE FAIREST ONE.